Andrew Staniland was born in Sheffield in 1959 and lives in London, where he works part time. His books so far have been self-published (poetry collections, narrative poems, prose-poem novels and plays).

titles by the author:

A Georgian Anthology
Letters Of Introduction (2018)
Playful Poems (2016)
Rhapsodies (2014)
The Perennial Poetry (2010)
Two Story Poems (2009)
Hymns, Films And Sonnetinas (2007)
New Poems (2006)
The Beauty Of Psyche (2005)
The Weight Of Light (2004)
Three Cine-Poems (1997)
Poems (1982-2004)
Four Plays (1994)

ANDREW STANILAND

THREE CINE-POEMS (1997)

published 2020 by
Andrew Staniland's Books

www.andrewstaniland.co.uk

front cover photos by the author

photo of the author by Robert Garbolinski

ISBN 9798642557679

Contents

WHITE RUSSIAN

London

1994

TEACHER: Try saying *the*.

                The class is blowing kisses
    At the young teacher.

TEACHER: Thank you.

                  Snake forks? Lip scoops?

TEACHER: One at a time.

            The word goes round the world,
Spluttering raspberries of aspiration.

A phone rings in the college office. Footsteps
Answer. Only a silence through the ceiling.
Home Office call? Routine investigation?
I am a student. I am very well.

Behind a plain facade, somewhere near Holborn,
Innocent tongues are tortured to speak English.

                    ❧

Free voices, like a conference of birds,
Babble their common bond, let loose from learning,
Fluent, excited.
           The shock of lunchtime sunshine.
Students walk sideways, backwards, laughing, tripping
Round swerving shoppers.
              Anna, Dominique
Duck from the noise, draw inward, make up secrets,
Nuzzling elbows, the rudder of a makeshift
Catamaran the crowded pavement buffets.

DOMINIQUE: We're going to a film tonight. Come with us.

ANNA: I can't.

DOMINIQUE: Just come.

ANNA: I'm busy.

DOMINIQUE: Someone...?

ANNA: No.

․

Echo of empty. Evening in an office.
Iron-grey carpets, bristle of the nylon
Static in sterile air. Hard white, a strip light
Stuttering. Unplugged rooms, blank screens, dead phones.
Half-written memos left on desks like omens,
The unsolved mystery of daily work.

One of the spectres in the sepulchre,
Anna shakes waste bins in a fat black sack.
Brown apple, sweet foil, tissues, shreds of letters,
Sandwich rind. Crack of cartons, rush of tumblers,
The bin bag sweating slops of slimy coffee.
She stretches a fresh one, billows it. Next bin.

Leo, the only man, locks sprays, cloths, buckets
In a long cupboard. Older shadows of
The students, the other cleaners claim coats, clatter
Chattering down the stairwell. Anna waits.
Her small ball of a boss, grey beard, red smile,
Digs a brown note roll from a droopy pocket,
Counts her pay, clamps her fingers in a fist.

․

Frayed leek stalks, boxes' angles. Anna swings
A plastic bag that twists and spins in sync
With the easy pleasure of the afternoon.

A man strolls closer, ups his eyebrows, grins,
Measures her waist, her legs.
                    She looks away,
Frowns at her own reflection in the glass
Chemist's display. Her ghost face drifts across
The glossy beauty products on display.

․

Pine squares so close the room looks like a chessboard.
Sparrowy waiters edge along the lines,

Arrowing trays like toy planes. Crisp fan pancakes,
Palettes of curries, yellow anthills of rice.

Hearts against tables, couples lean to meet,
Eyes miming. Steepled hands, a common prayer.
The noise of talking is their private space.

Anna snaps poppadoms, her spine birch-straight,
A glimmer of makeup, hair tied loosely up.
Her old-world elegance, in jeans and sweater,
Is style from nothing, by her definition,
Like the simplicity of Taoist painting,
One quick black brushstroke, mountain, blossom, painter.
She glances at the couples crowded round her,
Their easy love, these matching pairs of strangers,
Not opposites, not magnets. Familial
Soul lines. She looks at her companion.

Philip wears jeans and a sweater too, too neatly,
Haunted by the week's habit of a suit.
Freckled, bare eyelids under wisps of ginger,
Boyish and mild. The dial of his face
Is set to sensitive. Perhaps he is.
Nobody knows unless you show it.
                                        Anna
Pans a gold sludge of lentils with a poori.

PHILIP: She's an accountant. Big firm in the City.

ANNA: Who's the top earner?

PHILIP: She is.

ANNA: Is she married?

PHILIP: Divorced.

ANNA: Like mine.

PHILIP: Oh, really? Any children?

ANNA: A son.

PHILIP: It must be hard.

ANNA: It's typical.

PHILIP: What's her profession?

ANNA: Same as me.

PHILIP: A student?

ANNA: Engineer.

PHILIP: Oh, I… Good for you, I mean,
            We need some women engineers.

ANNA: There's thousands.

PHILIP: Hardly.

ANNA: Of course!

PHILIP: I'm serious. Not here.

ANNA: Really?

PHILIP: It's true. We're less advanced than you!
            A good skill for your sister, though, back home.
            Now, I mean.

ANNA: When the country falls to pieces?

PHILIP: No, when the private sector's taking off.

ANNA: That's a nice thought.

PHILIP: When people see a profit…

ANNA: They snatch it and they run! Like flies round shit,
            Vultures with black moustaches, dealing-stealing,
            Gangs on the streets…

PHILIP: Which city's this?

ANNA: Tbilisi.

PHILIP: You're Georgian?

ANNA: Russian.

PHILIP: Right… You said the South.

A waiter lifts a ziggurat of dishes,
Hands them hot flannels rolled in steamed-up plastic.

PHILIP: The civil war, against Abkhazia,
            I thought the Russians fought against the Georgians?

ANNA: The army fought.

PHILIP: Of course, but...

ANNA: Think of chaos.
           Double it. Home...

PHILIP: You're lucky you've escaped.

ANNA: Sometimes when people ask me where I'm from,
           I tell them I'm Italian.

PHILIP: Why not!

ANNA: They always speak Italian! Do you?

PHILIP: No. A few phrases. *Where is my hotel*?

ANNA: I'd love to go there.

PHILIP: Yes, it's beautiful.
           Possibly we could, if...

ANNA: I'll tell you why.
           I can't be who I am. Just me.

PHILIP: I'm sorry?

ANNA: I'm Anna the Russian! Well...

PHILIP: I understand.

Timid money. The bill is face down. Philip
Is quick, as if he thinks that she'll compete.
He looks but doesn't tell, unfolds his wallet.

PHILIP: It's on my card. Don't worry.

ANNA: Yes, of course.

PHILIP: It must be really hard how you survive.

&

Philip's black Golf curves in by Anna's house.
He clicks the engine off. They sit in darkness,
Ending the evening, quietly, unhurried.
Heads tilt and pass, a cheek kiss, friends' goodnight.

He grips her shoulder blades, twists round the wheel,
Mouth open for her lips, instinctive, plaintive.
Anna jerks back, firm hands a fence against him.
A rocky cliff edge splits the ground between them.

PHILIP: I'm sorry, maybe we need more time to...

ANNA: No.

The chairs' arm pads are bearded, foam tongues leer,
Official statements in an antechamber
Of the world outside, the greying white walls stained
By tidemarks.
            Fear shrinks lungs, a fear of fear,
Its false betrayal, flaws of innocence
Exposed, uprooted meanings. Which is which?
Exile and home. Thighs glue to seats' green plastic,
Hands nest like fledglings, feet on English land.

Stark faces, like a missing persons file,
Stare at the numbers ticking off the queue,
Their temporary state identities.
Nerve needles flicker. Masks of memories
Surface like skulls through skin. In the stagnant silence
Alien souls await their judgement.
                                Anna
Looks at her watch, her book's black language. Thoughts
Peck at a phrase, then scatter like scared gulls
Into the white wind of a wintry sky.

His desk, her checkpoint, is totemic. He
Is friendly, not to her, inquisitive
As if of someone else, a fantasy
Of questioning a tiny oval photo
Next to a vase of newly sharpened pencils.
Anna's voice is a bad ventriloquist.
He cleans his ear, amusingly perplexed.

OFFICIAL: Your English should be perfect soon.

ANNA: I hope so.

    The silence as he reads her file. The lacquered
    And gold-nibbed ink pen scratching secret notes.
    The frown, the sniff, before he primes his stamp.

OFFICIAL: Six months extension.

        Blue date on her visa.

           *

    She licks an ice cream, conquering the peak
    Of Primrose Hill. Which flag should she plant on it?
    Russian or British? A blind smile as she tilts
    Towards the yellow whiteness of the sun,
    High overhead, floats in it and they're talking,
    A one-to-one discussion in its heat,
    This wonderfully witty English sun.
    She knows now how the soul can shine so brightly,
    How it feels to be timeless, to taste light.
    She knows the sun is happy when she's happy.

    A visor of her fingers shields her eyes
    Surveying the soft cityscape spread south,
    Its mountain range of office blocks and steeples,
    St. Paul's to Chelsea, dreamy in a haze
    Of mauve fumes, distance blessing it as peaceful.

           *

    A hallway payphone, padlocked box tattooed,
    Flex peeling. In the vortex of a call,
    Anna curves, concentrating, where she is
    Superimposed, confused. Her Senegalese
    Neighbour slides past her to the bathroom.

NEIGHBOUR: Sorry.

The earpiece is as hot as unclean breath,
The terse familiarity of Russian
Like the blurred echo of an old typewriter.
She tussles to speak, a wrestling match of voices
She loses. Line fizz. Distant tears of home.
Her forehead wrinkles, better not to say,
Pretend to know. The call clicks dead. The toilet
Flushes. Too late to get back to her room.

NEIGHBOUR: All right?

ANNA: All right.

NEIGHBOUR: That's why we're here.

ANNA: I know.

&

After the fashion show, the empty stalls.
The judge holds out his hand to Valentine,
Like a bud springing through the stubbly bark
Of an old oak tree. Windows bang. March storms.

She speaks. A colour coding of emotions
Confessing, through the filter of her face,
White words engraved in light along the screen.
The judge nods.
                Jamie reads. A twitch of impact
Dances in Anna's eye. She looks at him,
Slouched in his seat, his swept-back S of hair
Washed for the evening, slightly crooked nose.
His profile, smoothed by gazing up, basks in
The film's reflected glory.
                            Jamie feels
A tingle in his cheek, the touch of seeing.
His sense of self, suspended by the film,
Stiffens, a sense of Anna next to him.
He lands his hand, as lightly as by chance,
Onto her knee.
                As if it was a hornet,
She knocks it clear, knees tight, and stares securely

Straight at the screen.
                          The film plays on its own.

                              ❧

A thumb-pinned Canaletto hides the wall,
Shoes hide the floor in Dominique's small room.
Black coffee cools in *I love London* mugs.

DOMINIQUE: It sounds completely crazy.

ANNA: Worse than crazy.

DOMINIQUE: You can't go back.

ANNA: I wish...

DOMINIQUE: If I was you,
        Really, I'd get my visa set in concrete!

ANNA: It's not so simple.

DOMINIQUE: Yes, it is. Get married.

ANNA: No, not for that.

DOMINIQUE: Why not?

ANNA: It's wrong.

DOMINIQUE: It's normal.

ANNA: I won't. It's what they think, *You Russian women,*
        You're husband hunters, all you want is money!
        They tell me to my face, as though it's kind,
        Our hearts are ice, we'll sell our souls for visas.
        It's such an insult.

DOMINIQUE: No one thinks you're like that.

ANNA: It's racist.

DOMINIQUE: Anna, that isn't what I meant.

ANNA: I know, but...

DOMINIQUE: Fall in love!

ANNA: Like that?

DOMINIQUE: Like me.
          I fall in love with someone every day!

ANNA: I'd have to meet the right man.

DOMINIQUE: What's the problem?
          They're queuing!

ANNA: No.

DOMINIQUE: I've seen them!

ANNA: They're the wrong ones.

DOMINIQUE: Surely there's one you fancy?

ANNA: Not to marry.
          That's a mistake I won't make twice.

DOMINIQUE: You haven't!

ANNA: In Georgia.

DOMINIQUE: Tell me, tell me!

ANNA: It was stupid.
          A teenage marriage.

DOMINIQUE: Really?

ANNA: We're old-fashioned.

DOMINIQUE: It was to teach you. Now you'll choose the right
                                              one.
ANNA: He'd think I only loved him for his passport.

DOMINIQUE: He'll love you. He won't care.

ANNA: I'd think so too.

DOMINIQUE: Anna, we've all got mixed-up needs and reasons.
          That's life.

ANNA: I always know when something's wrong.
          Maybe that's something wrong with me.

DOMINIQUE: Of course not.
          Maybe it's me who doesn't know. I love you,
          I want you to take root here, like a rose!

ANNA: Dominique!

DOMINIQUE: Like a perfect English rose!

ANNA: Will you go back to France?

DOMINIQUE: I'll stay if you stay.

ANNA: You're lucky. You can choose.

DOMINIQUE: No need to marry.
          I'll have a hundred lovers. English men!

ANNA: You wouldn't!

DOMINIQUE: No? I like them more than you do.
          The problem is, they all like you more than me!

ANNA: That isn't true! There's Mike.

DOMINIQUE: He's just a boyfriend.

ANNA: He's nice.

DOMINIQUE: He's mine! I'm joking. Have I told you
          The story of my aunt, my mother's sister?
          As pretty as porcelain, pursued like crazy.
          She always falls in love with married men,
          Happily married.

ANNA: Do they leave their wives?

DOMINIQUE: Never.

ANNA: That must be why she falls in love.

&

Cloud muscles, classical in clarity,
A jumbo rules along them like a thumb.
Anna stands still. A woman thuds against her.
They sheer off with annoyed apologies.

She slips out of the crowd into a space
Against a sun-warmed wall. The narrow sky's
Blue and white jigsaw, the pearl grey of the plane.
Where is it flying? Moscow? Rome? New York?

A lost millennium in dusty fields,
A pious peasant woman stops her hoeing,
Straightens her back and stares in divination
At the sky's sign, a migrant flight of heron.

PATRICK: Tomb of the Unknown Sculptor.

> Crinkled concrete.

PATRICK: No wonder he's unknown.

> A bowl of grass,
> Shaved for the summer, yellowing, dips down
> To scrub, like screens wheeled round a patient's bed
> At pan time, round a morbid pond's lead plate.
>
> Simmering on the slope is a mass life class,
> Eyes shut and ears plugged, skin as white as veal.

ANNA: How can they be so stupid?

PATRICK: Years of practice.

> Tall trees, top branches quick to catch the breeze,
> Cordon the park in pastoral illusion
> A silver ribbon of the city glints through.

PATRICK: Hey, have you been to Highgate Cemetery?

ANNA: No.

PATRICK: Have you heard about it?

ANNA: Is it famous?

PATRICK: Fairly. Come on, I'll show you round, it's great.

> He speeds her past a booth of guides and postcards,
> Up a dark alley of the dead, all sleeping.
> They laugh at the inscriptions' deathless verse,
> The etiquette of grief.
>   Lopsided headstones
> Lurch, an ironic Bacchanalia,
> Uprooted urns, an angel's broken nose,
> A thorny coil, a dripping shroud of ivy,
> Mossy saplings thrusting for sunlight. Life's
> Fertility triumphant over death's
> Heaven. A cycle of the soul on earth.

The path leads to a crossroads. Anna shrieks.
Karl Marx's tomb. A schoolboy grin from Patrick.

ANNA: He's buried here?

PATRICK: Surprise?

ANNA: He's like a lion!

An iron mane, a constipated glower.

ANNA: Like Nelson's Column!

PATRICK: Maybe it was spare.

They stroll through shadows from a catacomb
Of trees. Not chaperoned by strangers, Anna
Is Orpheus ascending. One wrong look?

Safe in the sun. A dentist's business plaque,
Personal callers only, a marble teddy
Mourning a tiny grave, a grand piano,
Old photos sealed like violets in amber,
An actress in her last romantic role.

PATRICK: A cup of tea? My flat's just up the road.

ANNA: I can't, no.

PATRICK: Well, a cafe in the village?

ANNA: I've got some homework, sorry.

PATRICK: Can I call you?

ANNA: Just as a friend.

PATRICK: All right. At least you've told me.

❧

A teabag turns to parchment in the saucer.
Dregs cold in the cup. A reflex of her fingers
Folding the wrapper of a chocolate. Square,
Triangle, square.
                  She watches the rough rushes
Of faces flicker past the cafe window,

Strangers, their lives opaque and distancing,
A few spliced seconds in her frame of thought.

Always a window. In the heat of meeting
A man, a glass partition keeps her cool,
Stops his invasion.
                    Till the casement opens
In the white tower. Not for Dominique's
Light-hearted love. A darkness of the spirit
Storming her senses, sacred all-transforming
Love, with its sudden presence in her heart,
As real as a fist.
                    An Anna-fantasy?
As likely as a miracle in England?
No, it still happens, rarely, absolutely,
Except to her.
                    Is there some mechanism,
A faulty valve, not working in her heart?
Or a lack of space? A room of red brocade
Where the shy princess can practise her new dance steps
Alone, without her brothers sniggering.
Is that what her ideals are? Older brothers
Stopping her dreams from dancing.
                                    Self-absorbed
Unbuttoning, a sexual abeyance,
Eyes on their clothes' two islands on the carpet.
Rolling off socks can never look romantic,
The way she's sitting makes her breasts seem small.
It's simple, practical. A hooded lamp's
Soft footlights on the bed. Skin, bone and shadow
Shrugging together...
                        No, it still feels wrong.

٭

Beauty is blossoming from the Goddess. Anna
Is gleaning, a wire basket in her elbow,
The reddest early apples from a box.
A young man veers his trolley round an aisle,
Clipping a carousel of cut-price biscuits.

He sees her, stares, unable to resist,
A perfect stranger, *La Sylphide* in Safeway.

She senses it, a glaring, like cold breath
Goosing her neck, and turns. A girl with nose rings,
A young man quickly bundling tomatoes,
A mother whining. Anna damps her instinct,
Searches for ripe bananas in a rack.

He looks again, discreetly bagging mushrooms.
Her lightness, of another world, he envies,
Seeing the female secret of his soul.

&

Curled on her bed alone, the radio,
A foetal sonar of her mother's heart,
Is playing from the Proms, Rachmaninov,
His Second Symphony, a song of exile
Gleaming like beaten copper in the firelight
Of home.
  Her mother, girlish for a moment,
Stirring adventures from her own crushed hopes.
Her mother's mother, deaf and loud, disgusted
At Anna living in the West. Her sister's
Sorrowful eyes. *You're free. I've got my son.*
I'm happy for you. Three-year-old Alexei,
Showing him maps, a globe. He wouldn't listen,
He wanted her to play with his new train.
Her father fussing. *Don't trust English men.*
Eat sensibly. Don't waste your money. Write!
The same unspoken thought in all their hearts.
Leave us behind.
  The lucky émigré
Is homesick for the noise in their cramped flat,
The kitchen smells, the steam of wet boots drying,
The chatter she can understand just hearing,
Not concentrating.
  Swollen by the music,
Her heart is streaming hot sad happy tears.

One for each mile? An overwhelming love
She is only free to feel so far away.

⋅⋅⋅

A field of purple furrows. Orange hills.
A circle-face, vast eyes, a shouldered scythe.
As though he's dancing, left foot on the neck
Of a brown scarecrow-brother. Is he dead?

GICA: What do you think?

DOMINIQUE: Fantastic!

ANNA: Interesting.
        Like a Chagall.

DOMINIQUE: Is there a story?

GICA: Sort of.

He plucks another from a giant's wallet,
Props it against the table. Lilac night,
A fringe of twigs, white flecks. A sun-sized star
With crooked spikes between a crescent moon's
Garlanded horns.

ANNA: What's this one called?

GICA: *The Lovers.*

DOMINIQUE: It's so romantic.

ANNA: I prefer the first one.

GICA: Why's that?

ANNA: It feels more finished.

DOMINIQUE: This one's finished,
        Isn't it?

GICA: Yes.

ANNA: I didn't mean... I'm sorry.

DOMINIQUE: They're both fantastic!

GICA: Thank you.

ANNA: Do you sell them?

GICA: A few. Through friends.

DOMINIQUE: You need publicity.
        A gallery.

GICA: I can't...

DOMINIQUE: Why not?

GICA: My visa.

ANNA: Where are you from?

GICA: Romania.

DOMINIQUE: She's Russian.

&

A dripping negative of summer, clouds
Curtaining light. It's treat time. Liberty,
Anna's ideal, a heaven of the senses.
She browses round the medieval courtyard,
Fingering silks, a peacock's turquoise tail.
She is a lady of the rarest taste,
So rare it stops her spending.
                              A feminine
Civilisation. Gauze bows' floating wings.
Strong fragrances of strawberries and roses,
Odours of leather. Glass cubes, golden strings
Draped on green velvet. Thumb and finger copy,
Chaining the naked lily of her neck.

Light-footed up the stairs. Sleek dresses trellised
Like orchids round the panelled gallery.
From buttery to beige, from silk to satin,
She waltzes, an elated energy
Imagining a soft new feeling. Gica.

&

Squashed on a bench splashed white by pigeon painters,
Brown bag and cellophane as made-up napkins,

Dominique rabbits crisps, her second packet,
Anna, mouth wide, a war cry, bites a bap,
Its filling bulging out. The sandwich smiles.

DOMINIQUE: I've got a new idea.

ANNA: Oh dear...

DOMINIQUE: It's great.

ANNA: What is it?

DOMINIQUE: Problem solved. You'll fall in love.
          These English boys aren't good enough for you.
          We'll go to Paris.

ANNA: Dominique...

DOMINIQUE: I promise,
          Men there are more refined, they're sly, they're
                                        gorgeous...

ANNA: I'd have to be a masochist. No way!

DOMINIQUE: What's wrong?

ANNA: It's not the men, it's learning French,
          Starting again. I think my brain would burst.

DOMINIQUE: It's France's loss...

ANNA: What else is going on?

DOMINIQUE: We're meeting for a drink tonight.

ANNA: A pub?

DOMINIQUE: I know. We'll sit outside, unless it rains.

ANNA: Who's going?

DOMINIQUE: Mainly Mike's friends. They're all right.
          Maria, Gica, Steve.

ANNA: I might come later.

*

Glasses of lager gleam like amber streetlamps.
Cigarettes glow. Blue souls of smoke float up.

The city night is surging, swaggering,
Splintering light, its artificial stars.
Its noise menagerie is edging higher,
Metallic, in a vast black vat of heat.

Mike acts a myth out, that he says is true,
About a monkey and the Lottery.
He screeches, hops on haunches round a bench,
Slapping his shiny forehead. Dominique,
Quoting the old patristic paradox,
Squeals. She believes because it is absurd.

As quiet as their shadows in the darkness,
Anna and Gica sketch their past, the borders
Behind them of their disinheritance,
Like travellers outside a country inn
Comparing paths, the long walk up the valley,
The pass, the south peak, superstitiously
Silent about the mountain still to climb.

Dominique whispers to her monkey. Mike,
Chanting a chimp song, scampers up to Anna
And grabs her by the legs. That's what they do,
He tells her, she should watch more wildlife shows.

❧

His hair like rope, the coal mines of his eyes,
Used to outfacing beauty in his art,
His cheekbones, blood-red lips, a narrow beard
Sombre against his smile.
                              A flame in sunlight,
His after-image trembles in her vision.
He is an olive tree, as gaunt and virile,
Deep-rooted, tense and strong.
                              She can't sleep, sees
A stone hut, his, in creased brown hills, cool water
Hauled from a well, a plate of goat's cheese, grapes
From hillside vines, rough bread, an iron lantern
As evening's guide, a black sky soaked in stars.

21

A country unhurt by our century,
Where art is sacred, secret and austere,
A solitary work of oil on canvas,
Mastering the slow mysteries of earth.

ès

A mudslide of commuters oozes through
Ticket gates, snapped in two, like riot shields
Left in a line. The border guards have panicked,
Fleeing the flood home of humanity.

Black in black dust, mice rustle in the track well.
Contestants crowd imaginary doors.
The tunnel brings a wind first, then a blur,
Then capsules open, their sour saunas spill.

Flushed faces, full of sweat and rain, straps straining,
Stained jackets off the shoulder. Ties do back-flips,
Like Isadora's scarf for businessmen.
Umbrellas, hanging baskets in a hothouse,
Slop against bags of lunch-hour groceries.

Anna slips out, Olympian by habit,
Slaloming through the downsurge to the street.

ès

White liners on her forearm like a waiter,
Dragging a black sack down the corridor,
Office to office, emptying, renewing,
She hums into a corner cubicle.

A man is slumped, a pyramid of elbows,
Staring at two green screens. He swivels, grins.

ANNA: Sorry.

MAN: Tchaikovsky?

ANNA: Yes...

MAN: Which swan are you?

ANNA: The swan who cleans the bins.

                              He slews his chair.
          She clears the bin's crushed Coke cans, half-chewed burger.
          The chair swings round. His elbow pokes her buttocks.
          Anna jolts, jars her head against the desk.
          The man laughs.

MAN: Slapstick! Sorry, mustn't mock.

          She fumbles a new liner, near the doorway,
          Calf muscles twitching warnings.

MAN: What a job!
              The wrong profession for a pretty lady.
              You should be a receptionist, at least.

ANNA: That would be nice...

MAN: There must be some dark secret!

ANNA: No.

MAN: After hours? Cash in hand?

                                  His thumbs
          Grease fingertips, too close to where the bin goes.

MAN: You're Russian, aren't you?

ANNA: No, Italian.

MAN: Yeah, right, if someone heard me humming Elgar,
           I'd still swear I was Swiss!

                              The empty bin
          Swings in her hand.

MAN: The lady daren't bend over!
              What does the Home Office think? A pretty student?

ANNA: Mind your own business.

MAN: What's your name?

ANNA: Madonna.

MAN: I'll get you chucked out!

ANNA: Keep your fucking bin!

                                    ❧

Hugging the concrete parapet's protection,
Big pupils swamped and hectic, scared of blinking,
She stares down from the bridge, a teenage conscript
On sentry duty in a hostile country.

Wind from the river slicks her cheeks and hair.
The storm has drum-rolled north. Stray husks of rain
Speck the sluiced air, light-headed from the beating.

She huddles, the thunder of a bus behind her
Swaying across the bridge, the backs of buildings
Where enemies are hiding on the bank,
The callous beauty of the tide-washed water's
Platinum flare paths, rosaries of lamps.

Night's graphite grains the high lines of her cheekbones.
The ghostly omens of her worst emotions
Are waxy in the sodium.
                        It rains.

                                    ❧

Anna and Gica wander round the park's
Stone chalices, white fountains, clipped lawns, tripwires
And geometric flowers. Burnished keepers
Turf in a new bed, seasonally pretty,
Like implants of cosmetic surgery.

Strollers and rollerbladers pass them. Fields
Of baseball slope towards a minaret,
The mosque's dome in the west a setting sun.

A nervous curve of fur, surprised, surprised,
A squirrel fidgets, either food or fear,
Splays on a tree trunk, scavenges a bin.

ANNA: Maybe we'll see a wolf soon, if we're lucky.

GICA: The steppes of Regent's Park!

ANNA: You don't believe me?

    A she-wolf, streaked blonde, a taut Tartar smile,
    Lopes slowly, sleepily, from shade to shade,
    A bride of Genghis Khan, caged in the zoo.

GICA: Tell me the Thames has crocodiles.

ANNA: Just sharks.

    They laze against the hot rail of a bridge.
    A water meditation. The canal,
    A row of houseboats, vermicelli willows,
    A floating Chinese restaurant's pagoda.

ANNA: Gica... I love you.

    The water's green reflections, midges' mist.

GICA: Anna, you're very beautiful. I'm sorry.

    A duck dives through the upside-down mosaic.

GICA: If we were free, if ifs weren't ifs... You'd risk it?
             Really, you would? I wish I had your courage.
             No, I'm in love already, with the West.
             I want to be free to... Shit! I feel like Adam,
             The fall guy, saying no to Eve. I mean it.
             Where would we live? Tbilisi? Bucharest?
             We've made it, we can stay in paradise.
             I won't give up that chance. It isn't worth it.

    Primrose Hill is so near to them, it's hidden.
    She'd planned they'd share the view.
                                        A shrug's ellipsis.
    They walk back wordlessly, the zoo, the gardens,
    As though rewinding would erase the tape.

❧

Two steps behind her mother, kicking grit,
Thoughtful and tired, a girl trails a balloon.
The orange face-paint of a happy tiger,
Obsolete, smiles in schizophrenic stasis.

After they've passed her, Anna hides her face
In a tissue, snorts and spits tears in the gutter.
Only her ears aren't crying. Joke. More tears.

Parks are too painful. Streets are grey and sleepy.
Family snapshots show through windows. Plants,
An old brass music stand, a stained glass disc.

&a.

Stars' pinpoints, angels dancing, city-pale
Tatters of cloud. The moon, a crescent quarter,
Brightens, blurred yellow on the gaseous skyline.

Anna stops on the step, stares at the night's
Violent void, its light's serenity.
She turns to the house, a tall Victorian
Fallen from grace, its long sardonic face.

She flicks the hall switch. Nothing. A burnt-out bulb?
Hands paddle down the wall. The letter table
Bashes her shin to spite her, with a spurt
Of helpless hurt. She kicks a bike. Spokes jangle.
The stairs' light. Nothing. Not the bulb, the fuse.

Her knuckles rattle on the landlord's door.
No answer. It's the night he goes out drinking.
He'll blame her, belch beer in her foreign face,
Too drunk to find the cellar key.
                                    Is she
Jinxed? Is her bad luck bringing more bad luck?
A farce of fate? A blackout like back home,
But she's alone.
                    Her elbow cracks the doorframe.
She is a scapegoat of the darkness, cornered
In her room's fusty hole, the radio

And kettle dead and she too sad, too sour
To sleep it off.
         She fumbles to the bathroom,
Slams the door, bolts it, dowses for the taps.
Black water roars. Ghosts cloud up from the cauldron,
Crying. Her clothes are clammy.
                 Anna strips
And slides in through the steam that blots her pores.
The blind night water melts her weightless body.
She ducks through chutes of bubbles, senses swimming,
Hair billowing like grass.
            A secret cave's
Mineral pool, a font where names are lost,
An amniotic underworld. To drown?
Naked at midnight in a stony lake,
A trough of pig's blood at Eleusis.
                  Tears
Melt on her wet cheeks like a lustral oil.
She sinks again, stays under, stops her breath,
A childhood counting test.
           She chooses life
And springs up, spouting, fountaining. A dolphin,
Spirit and body, diving in the darkness,
Conjuring light in splashes, flipper wrists,
Waves from her hips.
          She crescents, floating free
In the hot bath, unknown in endless night.

                 ❧

The immigration office's crude concrete
Is like a threat of thunder. Anna waits,
A woman in a war zone's no man's land.

What does she want? What is she? What is hers?
Only what is a refugee's. Her self.

Are we rewarded when we do what's right?
Is she a criminal? What's wrong with working?

Strands stuck across his scalp, cigar-red skin,
Anubis annotates her fate, inspects her
Like trophy art. To be repatriated?

OFFICIAL: Six months extension.

Blue date on her visa.

❧

A chestnut veils the view from Richard's flat.
Rain rakes its ragged branches. Cars below,
Spray genies, fizz by, with their wipers' hand jive.

A tightrope walker with a wobbly tray,
He curtseys clumsily, but doesn't spill
The teapot, cups and saucers, biscuit bin.

He starts an album strumming from the speakers
And stands by Anna at the misty window.
Their damp jeans, ironed by the radiator,
Prickle their legs. Their hands on the white sill,
Between small pots of cacti, chord its keyboard.
He's seen the rain. He looks at her instead,
The dark warmth in her eyes, her dog-leg smile.

It's easy when a storm decides things for you,
Lips drawn into the orbit of a kiss.

A CHILD OF GOD

London

1995

Somebody starts it, mystery misquoted,
Misunderstood, a marble orthodoxy
Sold to the world.
                    Our own unique adventure.
The steady state of being what we see,
Simple self-truth, translucence, beauty, bliss,
The heart dimension of the universe.
By definition, what is absolute
Is absolutely tolerant, is you.

Even an Englishman can get enlightened.
He meets the masters, tries the tricks and teachings,
Like Alexander learning from the sadhus
The secrets of their freedom and their power.

A slim stream seems embarrassed by its valley.
Did I do that? By running to the lake.
A silk sleeve's graze will rub away a rock
In time, a granite clock of transformation,
While Brahma blinks.

❧

                    Green shoots are small grass Samsons
Whose temple earthquakes crack the concrete garden
Of a Fifties semi. A fault line in a window,
Black leaf sludge, dust veins, powdered pebbledash
Rubbed by the silk and stream of wind and rain.

A football clangs the dustbin. Two crouched boys,
Video-urchins, mount a daring rescue
Under the window, snatch it, snigger, run.
Whose house is it? *Dunno. The timelord Zorg's
When he's not cyber-fighting.* Back in play,
Their running commentary calls a crowd.

❧

The truth is true through its own trinity,
Who speaks, who's spoken to and the spent breath

33

Of speaking it. An actor knows a play,
A ghost on paper, has the most to say
As sheer experience.
                    His song of seeing,
As sharp as sure, his tenor slowly rising,
Translates it for them, surfing on their silence.

PAUL NIRVANA: I am Divine, I am the Infinite,
            An emanation of the Eminence,
            The central Supersoul, in incarnation
            In Ealing, in this body, on this Earth,
            For you. And just like you! Right? That's the power,
            The purpose. Why I tell you, worship me.
            The eye of worship sees in my perfection
            A picture of your own supreme potential.
            And what you worship is what you become.
            I see it growing in you, feel the glow.
            You'll be the cosmic kings, the star princesses!
            Why not? It isn't difficult to be
            Divine. Look in *The Book Of Consolations*.
            Devotion and divinity are equal.
            The more devoted you become to me,
            The more divine you are.

                    The guru's garden,
Sunflowers staring at the sun, his seedlings
Are growing to him, grounded in his presence.
A circle of seven, an Egyptian number,
They are the stones the builders have rejected,
Building Jerusalem, a new Atlantis.

The grimy lounge is Merlin's grotto. Sheets
Drape from the walls like laundry day, arcana
In poster paint. A nature table's magic
Branches, whorled pebbles, seeds, a moulting feather,
A blue glass pyramid, a dinner gong.

Sunk in the wheezy suction of the sofa,
Mary and Linda feel all-seeing eyes

Lasering through the clothes of their pretences,
A barn owl watching mice.

NIRVANA: I want to teach you
            How to escape the living death-in-body.
            Break free! From thought-illusions, from the system,
            The brain-drugs, blind beliefs, the stupid rules
            They tell you. Throw the switch, it's countdown,
                                            blastoff,
            Your own ascension into Total Mind.
            Why do you think a corpse's hair still grows?
            The natural lifespan of a human being
            Is centuries. So how come no one knows?
            It shows you how much censorship there is.
            The Silent Tyranny! The Government,
            The media, the Church. It's like a car.
            They make their money out of obsolescence,
            Designed decay. They kill us! Cancers, stress,
            The sicknesses of wealth. And poverty.
            Death is the weapon of authority!
            Without it, why would anyone obey them?
            In higher cultures, in the Golden Age,
            The ancients lived for ages, hence their name.
            The Mayas knew. *The truth of the Immortals
            Is immortality.* Just think about it.
            They're still alive today, in northwest China,
            The Amazon, the Himalayas, Wales.
            I've met them, they're amazing, all those years.
            Just think how wise you'd be, how much you'd
                                            know.
            But people don't believe it! Midget minds,
            Trapped in their tiny egos, so afraid...

&

The master's chair is a winged leather throne
Scratched by a past-life cat. A white paint spittle
Stipples its arms. Nirvana shuts his eyes,
Straightens. His heels are hooked, his knees are flying.
The guru-grasshopper chants an astral mantra.

Their slow minds sink, like twilight, to a tape's
Guttural tug. The sound of gravity
Throbs in the room. His *Mind Of God* technique.

The Earth's etheric spheres, like Saturn's rings,
Red at the core, the heart sphere, brown, green, blue,
The biospheres, then lilac, yellow, white,
The spiritual stratospheres. An opal
Seen by an astronaut. Nirvana, soaring,
Casually glances from his capsule window
And takes a snapshot. Telling will enlarge
The vision of his mission.
                              Roger judders.
A chrysalis of skin that wants to burst.
It's why he feels so wrong. The pressure deepens.
A snake charm sends a serpent up his spine,
Jerking his neck. His pupils, out of sight,
Stare into space, into a black and blue
Cranial cosmos.
                      A skeleton of suet,
Keith has collapsed. He wonders what it means,
Suddenly thinking, *Sherlock Holmes*. He wanders
In a green fog of spectral iridescence.
A lady calls. A silver image of
Madame Blavatsky passes through a wall.
He follows. Crates, his old job, all the gang
Loading a lorry. Now he understands,
No going back, he's safe here.
                                      Linda smiles
And shines. A disembodied sense of being.
Her breath flows like the sea. The sea is light.
She is a seal, an angel of the sea,
Flopping into it.
                        A shimmering white lotus
With giant petals is an inner stage.
Its footlights are a thousand temple flames,
Its stalls and circles all the universe.
Mary choreographs it. Supple, naked,
Her master and his consort's dance is tantric,

Thigh-balancing, on one foot, on a dwarf.
Their tongues loll out, four hands in formal quarters,
An ecstasy of true tranquillity.
Her hips balloon. A star has been created.
It's ritual, not physical, of course.
She'll tell it to her Mom next time she writes,
Marked, *Private. Not For Husband.*
                              Long legs like
A zimmer frame in front of a low armchair,
His head bent in an air guitarist's nod,
Werner jets back to Düsseldorf. He jokes,
At ease behind the lectern, tells the crowd,
My friends, this is the most extraordinary
Epoch in history. It is unique.
Two thousand years of order are beginning,
A spiritual world, a healthy planet.
We are the leaders of this transformation,
The rods, transducing energy to light...
Too stunned to clap, his speech has changed their lives.
A prophet's daydream. After it he'll feel
Exhilarated, vital.
                    Jill is thinking,
But with incredible intensity,
About her dinner. Thoughts fly up like birds
Scared by an engine digging a new road.
Her shaved skull, like a Disney fawn's new fur,
Makes her child-face immaculately truthful.
An eye flicks open. No one else is looking.
She gazes at her guru, meditates
On the still flame, her prince in exile.

                              Werner
Brings in a tray with beakers of hot water.
They sip it, tell their pilgrims' tales. Nirvana
Sits separately, smiles indulgently.
They are his flock of foundlings, superhumans
Stumbling up the hill to Zarathustra.

ROGER: I felt this whoosh of energy. Amazing.

JILL: An angel yanked your ponytail!

ROGER: You saw it?

MARY: When I was eight, I saw an angel.

JILL: Really?

WERNER: Can you describe it?

MARY: Sure. It was colossal,
            Like a glass office block, in so much sun
            It was one huge invisible reflection.

JILL: The state you must have been in.

MARY: Arizona.

WERNER: The desert! You can see the energies,
            Even in films.

ROGER: And I grew up in Leeds!

MARY: Only my Mom believed me. It was bad...

WERNER: Was it a native spirit?

MARY: Absolutely.

KEITH: The Dharma Master in *The White Oak Lectures*
            Says we can see two classes of angelics.
            The basic sort, the ectoplasmic angel,
            Is like a nature spirit or a guide.
            Guardian angels, forest angels, right?
            The archon angels are less space-specific,
            On more akashic planes. They're really vast,
            Like channelling a planet!

WERNER: So you mean
            Mary's angel would be a basic...?

MARY: Hey!

WERNER: Isn't a native spirit...?

MARY: Listen up,
            He was gigantic.

WERNER: Yes, but...

MARY: It's the truth!
          He was very, very special.

ROGER: Werner, please,
          It's Mary's angel.

WERNER: Sorry.

MARY: Right.

ROGER: That's better.

JILL: Why was it bad, though?

MARY: Angels make you lonely.
          No one else saw it, no one wanted to.
          I lost my friends, I couldn't... It was weird,
          Like living somewhere wrong, not being real.
          It wasn't till I... till my guru found me...

WERNER: I was saved too.

JILL: I'm lucky. Dad's a Druid.

MARY: Suddenly, all the things I'd always known...

ROGER: Me too. It's great, so normal, sitting here
          Discussing angels like they're on the telly!

KEITH: They would be if the wavelength was the same.

ROGER: My second year at college...

WERNER: Television,
          Telepathy, yes?

JILL: Channels!

KEITH: Simple state
          Electropsychics.

ROGER: Right. I studied Blake,
          Serious angel scene, I mean. The tutor,
          When someone quoted Swedenborg and said
          She'd had a similar experience,
          He was, like, what's that smell? No social comment?
          Odd guy, a Dylan freak.

                  The doorbell chimes,
          Three times, a sign to answer. Jill is nearest

And jogs out. An adventure on the threshold.
The circle listens. Guests are sent by God.

&

RICKY: Is Linda Staples here?

JILL: Who wants to see her?

MRS. STAPLES: Dear God, they've shaved the poor girl's head!

MR. STAPLES: Shush, dear.

RICKY: Can we come in?

JILL: Who are you?

RICKY: We're her friends.

LISA STAPLES: Ricky!

RICKY: Just let me...

LISA: We're her family.

JILL: I'm Jill. I'm pleased to...

MR. STAPLES: Now!

RICKY: Make way for Christ!

They ask for guidance in the hallway. Silence
Listens to silence listening.
                    Eyes shut
And palms out, Ricky, Lisa's boyfriend, is
An exorcist, inched forward by her parents'
Nails jabbing him, their rabbit punches.
                              The lounge.

&

MRS. STAPLES: Dear Lord! It smells like Satan in a brothel.

LINDA: What do you want?

MR. STAPLES: We've come to take you home.

LINDA: Ha! Home to hell!

MRS. STAPLES: The word...

RICKY: That's how it works.
            Classic inversion.

MR. STAPLES: Linda, please, we love you.

LINDA: You don't!

MRS. STAPLES: Of course we do, our little baby.

LINDA: I'm not a baby.

MRS. STAPLES: That's what you think.

MR. STAPLES: Mother!

LISA: Listen, Linda, I know you'll say you're fine.

RICKY: That's why we're here.

LISA: We're standing on a hill…

RICKY: A green hill far away.

LISA: It means that we
            Can see the danger you're too close to see.

RICKY: It's like a dream. It seems completely real.

LISA: Till you wake up.

LINDA: I've woken up already,
            Not from a dream, a nightmare. You!

                                    Her father,
        Reining his snorting wife against her will,
        Is Ben Hur on his chariot.

RICKY: One question.
            Would you be saying all these hurtful things
            If this was really what you think it is?

LINDA: All right, I'll tell you. Paul says, *Give forgives*.
            He shows us how to soak our souls in love.
            It's more than prayers or hymns. It really works.
            But I feel guilty.

RICKY: Good. That's very good.

LINDA: I still can't hate you any less. I hate you!

Her mother has a vision. Torchlit dungeons,
The Inquisition's tools. She ticks a list.

LISA: It's Satan talking.

MR. STAPLES: When you're home…

RICKY: The thing is,
          It's all right being angry…

MR. STAPLES: Not with us.

RICKY: But dancing with the Devil…

MR. STAPLES: With damnation…

RICKY: It's cutting off your soul to spite your face.

LINDA: You want to kill my soul!

MR. STAPLES: We want to save you.

    Nirvana lifts a finger, like the wing beat
    Of a bored butterfly. The room is silent.

NIRVANA: Swallow asks Camel, *What's your word for summer*?
          The camel answers, *Desert*.

LISA: What?

NIRVANA: The point is,
          If Linda wants to leave with you, she can.
          The choice is this, direct experience
          Or dogma, tested truth or superstition,
          Freedom or fear.

LINDA: I want to stay with you.

LISA: Think of your family.

NIRVANA: Biology!
          She's found her soul's eternal family.

LINDA: A family that loves me!

RICKY: Christ on High,
          Drive out the Demon Kingdom from this house!

    He prowls the lounge, as though his eyes have failed,
    Chopping the air with stiff karate crosses,

A strain of evangelical Tai Chi.
He hisses, gurgles, grunts. An armpit halo
Of unbathed odours sends the demons reeling.

Nirvana's eyelids are thin slits, to see more,
More mind, more light. He circuits thumb and index,
Building his energy, till spirit-spheres
Beat in the air, like moths drawn to a fight.
He checks his chakras, the axis of his orbit,
Thinks of a force field beaming from his chest.

His devotees septuplicate him, sitting
In the same state, although not so serenely,
Dodging the halo, chanting fresh air mantras,
Staring at Ricky like a monk's first skull.

MR. STAPLES: Grab her!

MRS. STAPLES: You little maggot...

                         Hair, arms, wool,
They drag her by the handful. Linda leaps,
Shocked by their grasp, like cattle prods, and snarls
At years of smacking, smacks back, jabs a ribcage.
They slap her face.
                    The tangled family
Is a gigantic blood-mad octopus
Slithering on the sofa, yanking, squelching.

Jill hops on top, chokes Ricky with his collar.
Keith necklocks Lisa. Roger, Werner, Mary
Quarter the octopus.
                     Nirvana watches
With a calm smile, as if he's read the ending
Or doesn't need to, abstinent, accepting.
A guru's first rule. Never get involved.

It is a tug of war, a medieval
Cup tie, Crusaders versus Heretics,
For Linda. Feeble fists flail. Beakers spill
Warm water on the carpet.
                          What's the score?

Six against four. The weight of sacred numbers.
The losers leave, a doctrine of excuses
Ready. At least they've not lost Lisa too.

MR. STAPLES: You'll break your mother's heart.

MRS. STAPLES: So selfish, selfish...

LINDA: I'm not your daughter. Understand? I'm dead!

&

A ritual to welcome or expel.
An eager boyfriend dusts and rinses mugs
Before a first date. An abandoned wife
Scrubs out the stains of violence and failure.
Lady Macbeth does housework.
                                        Heal the space.
They soothe its totems, smooth the paint-starched sails.
Cushions are slapped in shape. The true alignment
Of chairs placates the tidy-minded gods.

Mary wraps arms round Linda, tries to root her,
Dilated, deafened by adrenalin.

&

NIRVANA: *For I am come to set a man at variance against his father,*
          and the daughter against her mother... And a man's foes
          shall be they of his own household...
          Exactly as I told you, word for word,
          Even their own predictions fall against them.
          Out of the mouths of wolves, the trumpet call
          Of the new lambs. It's like the Great Succession.
          Time is a spiral, prophecies return.
          But we won't blame them, they're the messengers,
          The infantry, that's all, sent here to show us
          The forces of control have been alerted,
          The days of persecution have begun.
          But those who rule by fear are ruled by fear.
          They're scared of us, that's why they want to stop us.

They can't, but watch them try. We'll blow it open!
The whole conspiracy, the simple secret
Censored for centuries. We're living it!
Look at the Church. It's impotent, it's empty.
Just bishops, books and buildings. Cups of tea.
Religio piscorum. End of story.
Two thousand years? Two thousand light years now!
It's like... How many people worship Zeus?
What happened to the Titan Gods before him?
Precession of the equinoxes, right?
The fate of Kronos is the fate of Christ.
It's the Third Law of Nature. Ages change.
And if a king won't die, he gets usurped.
New wine in new skins. Throw away the old.
New skins? That means new bodies, spirit bodies,
Bodies of light. Is it coincidence
We're sitting in this circle while the world
Hurtles towards a new millennium?
And not just any old millennium,
Celestial Year Zero, Cosmic Dawn,
An Equinoctial Millennium.
It means that light and dark are equal now.
It means the ultimate war at last. The Power
Of Revelation or Apocalypse?
Everyone thinks the Negative is winning.
The ozone layer, pollution, global warming,
Mad-cow disease, materialism, scratch cards.
It's like Arjuna on the battlefield,
He chooses Krishna rather than his armies.
Think what we're up against, the money-makers,
The military industry, the Church.
But we've got Krishna. We're the light. We'll win.
We're bound to. It's the Thirteenth Law of Nature.
If we just do the work. It's such a blessing
To be so necessary, so essential.
I'll tell you your reward, beyond belief,
Instant connection to the Mind of God.
Only the greatest sages gained this grace
Till now, till you. It's scientific too.

The way it works is, terminology
Is the technology. And we keep learning,
New tools, new truths. The modem of the mind,
The internet of consciousness. Let's test it.
It says, *I am the Way, the Truth, the Life.*
In other words, the I, the Self is God,
Which means the individual is free.
And they deny it. *It means blah blah blah...*
Interpretations of obedience.
But we can be objective, so we know...

❧

Three mattresses claim corners of the floor.
A shop rail for a wardrobe, suitcase drawers,
A dolphin poster on the floral wall.

A candle in a cave, book tilted to it,
Linda lies reading, studying the scriptures,
The Gnostic Buddha And The Wand Of Life
– A Secret World Religion For The Future
By Bronwyn Jones. She peels a page, new chapter,
Pets Are Our Native Spirit Guides.
                    Dear Mom.
Sprawled on a cartoon duvet, Mary scribbles
Sheet after sheet.
              The door yawns. Jill slips in,
Walpurgisnacht-like, naked as a goat,
Snub nipples, rungs of ribs, a gluey trickle
Dewing her thighs, a raw glint in the dimness.
She grins and lifts her eyebrows.
                    Linda's cue.
Her bookmark is a unsent postcard of
Crop circles. One hand claps the book shut. She
Pulls off her sweater, scruff-first, rubs her eyes,
Ruffles her hair, then plucks her jeans off too.
She is a goose, the blank slab of her belly.

❧

Nirvana's bedroom, smoked by sandalwood,
Is black, as black as Kali in a graveyard
At midnight.
            Only touch the mystery,
A blind taste test, like Semele or Psyche
Loving at night. It would be devastating
To see the naked guru's true dimensions.
Linda believes him, dreaming, as she feels
His greatness growing.
                        Breasts on bones, his chest
Is an ascetic's bed of nails. She sips
His spit's elixir, sucks his sacred breath
Like dragon fire.
                    They could be yin and yang,
Planets or gods, a cosmic union
Of anything immense and sexual,
In the imagination of the night.

He fills her void. She arches like an angel.
Her nerve ends send new pinpricks up her spine.
Shakti is Shekinah, the Shulamite
Sitting on Solomon.
                    The supine guru,
Under her straddle, lies as still as Shiva,
As though his slightest motion might explode
So much extraordinary energy
Whole galaxies would be obliterated.

She peaks. She is a penetrated priestess,
Garlanding with her own red rose the stone
Phallus a miracle of blood makes human.
Her flesh is foamy, hot, a shot of semen
Into her grotto.
                    And the miracle
Abates, from infinitely great to small.
It is beyond orgasmic. She feels blessed
To be his choice of chalice. As he says,
The vital pleasure is vicarious.
Some sit at gurus' feet, some sit on top
And some have gurus thrust upon them.

⁛

                       Awesome.
Their morning meditation changed the weather.
The day was so opaque, so grey, it seemed
Separate from the sacred, from the sun,
Under an endless uncarved block of cloud.
Then forty minutes' timeless transformation,
Like waking twice, a second chance, and whoosh!
A sky as blue as Krishna, bright and empty.
The power of pure mind or what he calls
Quantum causality.
                 A slide of light,
Its autumn angle yellowing the lounge,
Shows the sun's secret dust. Warm spirals dance.

NIRVANA: You're looking at the dust of Genesis,
           The golden particles of Demiourgos
           That transmigrate from skin to air to carpet.

Their breakfast is a bowl of rice and lentils,
Hot water and the guru's favourite,
A Mars bar.

WERNER: Do you think it's beneficial
           To drink your urine?

NIRVANA: It's a valid practice,
           From Ayur Veda, not to lose your fluids.
           It's mineral retention, technically.
           But we work from the source, the Mind of God,
           It's so complete, so absolutely total,
           You don't need candles when the sun shines!

WERNER: Right.

An instant answer moulded to his message,
His sutras are a soundbite for the soul.
The group relaxes, liquidates the thought.

KEITH: You want to add some flavour to your water!

WERNER: I want to get enlightened.

ROGER: Hey, in Thailand,
          This Buddhist guy, he's in the Government...

JILL: Really?

MARY: That's great.

ROGER: He drinks his guru's urine!

          Why did he say that? How could they refuse?
          Roger gulps dryly, waits to hear the teaching.

NIRVANA: It's all transmission, all totality.
          I hope he won't regret it, though. The guru.
          He's handing out a blueprint of his body,
          His secret code, in each secreted cell.
          What if it's used against him? Like black magic.
          It isn't worth it, when there's no real need.
          I give you pure transmission by my presence.

                          ❧

          Nirvana hunches at his old computer's
          Black window, taps a snowstorm, as amazing
          As Mozart, keying in to what he knows,
          His wisdom line.
                          The Goddess Astimante
          Dictates from Constellation Sirius
          The Bible of the New Millennium.
          It's less historical, more practical,
          The Third and Highest Testament, ascending
          From Law to Love to Unifying Truth.
          He's waiting for the sign of page 2000
          To publish it.
                          His letters tile the table,
          To New Age magazines, the Daily Mail,
          West Indian Prime Ministers, a film star.
          Thumbed books, his red corrections in the margins,
          Computer games, a tarot pack, his dental
          Impressions in old chunks of chocolate.

An early-warning aerial, his spine
Stiffens, a siren sounding through the fug
Of concentration.
                              As if fierce eyes are reading
Next to his neck. He swivels, faces an
Invisible intruder's ion-omens,
As if a thunderstorm had charged the air
Or the wind blown the window open. Static
Bounces between them, two magnetic poles.
His opposite, an awful force of Nature,
Anti-Nirvana.
                        Arch-Nirvana, slowly
Circling anti-clockwise, underchants
Overtones, paces crosses on the carpet,
Trips on a pile of trousers.
                                        On the mattress,
Black plasma, he can almost see it, twisting,
Eating the light. He anti-channels it,
Earthed through his socks, his fingertips conducting
The astral positive.
                              He feels its frenzy
Resisting him. Its power is a secret.
He can't expel it till he knows.
                                              His hands
Are drawn towards a diary. He fans it
Until he finds the date. The fifth of June.

The pressure drops. His ears pop. The hot room
Re-ionises, lightens.
                              Sweaty fingers
Stick to the book. His chakra-eye of judgement
Studies the date's blank page, its hole in time,
For motives for its malice.
                                        On the screen
The cursor blinks. The last word. *Misconception.*
A bird's claws scratch the roof like sacred leaves,
Whispering hoarsely. *Ad nil. Death is born.*

A migraine blows a fuse across his temples.
The Ancient Pain. He stumbles for his pills,

Whoops down a double dose and draws the dark
Red curtains, curls up in a foetal coil.

❧

Werner and Jill sift lentils, Cinderellas
Without a slipper or a ball to go to.

WERNER: Meditating is difficult for Germans.
         It's tragic, when we're famous for our mystics,
         Goethe and Nietzsche, Rilke, Beckenbauer,
         But now, as soon as we go deep, we find
         Our soul, our great Romantic heritage,
         Blocked by a wall of karma from the war.
         It makes the Iron Curtain seem like cardboard.

JILL: Wasn't that excellent? The channelling
         Must have been mega-major. Whoa!

WERNER: I mean,
         No one is innocent. It's like a new
         Original sin.

JILL: Did you die in the war?

WERNER: I think I was a Wehrmacht officer
         On the Eastern Front.

JILL: Hey!

WERNER: What?

JILL: That's so prophetic.
         Eastern!

WERNER: I don't...

JILL: That's why. It's India!

❧

They share their insights, like a talent show,
With marks from one to ten for mystic merit.

MARY: When you explained duality this morning
         As lack of love, not reaching out, when really

We're drowning in a unity of love,
I realised that's how I've lived my life,
That's why I've been so scared, like me-and-them,
And now it's changed. It's so amazing. Thank you.

KEITH: I had a dream last night. A king and queen,
Siamese twins, were sitting in a bath
Of steaming asses' milk, a Roman sauna,
Healing their royal suffering forever.
They were both me. Nirvana, you're the bath.

LINDA: This isn't... Well, it's not a dream. I'm pregnant.

ROGER: You're... Wow!

WERNER: That's really great.

KEITH: Congratulations.

WERNER: The first child of the future!

KEITH: Of the teaching.

ROGER: I'm jealous. Of the baby.

WERNER: It's a sign.
A kind of miracle.

ROGER: A child of light!

Mary and Jill are fish-mouthed, out-devoted,
Wise virgins on the pill, but fools are holy.

KEITH: When is it due?

LINDA: They said the fifth of June.

ROGER: Gemi...

The guru's glare is like a gorgon.
His heavy centre sucks in their attention.

NIRVANA: I raise the astral sword of Sirius.
The Higher Voice, the Voice of Power speaks.
Destroy destruction or it will destroy us,
Destruction in the womb! I swear by Merlin,
This beast you're bearing isn't just a baby,
You're earthing evil, a worm of antimatter

That hates our work, our circle. Linda, stop it,
Abort it. It's your sacred duty. It's
Your duty to our destiny, to keep
The positive alive. A time is coming,
The Passiontide of Gaia, seven days,
Seven great stages of her Panacea.
There will be earthquakes, hurricanes, tsunamis,
Seven volcanoes, city-swamping floods.
A brand-new range of mountains will erupt,
Rainforests in the desert. The sick soil,
Black rivers, tainted trees, the bitter air
Will be washed clean, like children in a carwash.
Nuclear sewage will be alchemised,
Radiopassively, by phased emissions,
To common elements. Their tanks, their guns
Will drown or melt or buckle. Total change!
No man-made waste, no overpopulation,
A necessary threshold of purgation,
But we'll survive. That's why we're working now,
Transfiguring to higher frequencies.
Think how humiliating being human
Is, getting hungry, shitting, growing old,
But we'll have bodies of our soul's perfection.
It's so amazing. We'll be flesh and blood
On an etheric plane. That's never happened!
Angels will guide us where we're safe, they know
It's vital we survive, so we'll be ready,
The founding fathers of a new mankind,
When a white city rises from the sea,
The once-and-future Nirvanopolis.
Even the great light-beings need us here,
Serving the Godhead in this earthly sphere...

❧

The most profound, most powerful soul-states
Seem easy, normal, till you leave their space,
The temple's solemn grounds.

53

                        Too loud, too fast,
The slapstick speed of street life surges round her.

Shop windows are an unwound roll of film.
A cafe's sweating glass, a boarded blank,
A grocer's dusty cans and wrinkled apples,
A launderette, its portholes sloshing storms,
A line of coats like ghosts for charity.
Linda is looking with a feather-naked
Amazonian's Stone Age stare. She counts
The fault lines of the flagstones for some calm.

Her lungs cringe at a nicotine-blue slipstream.
She sees a neck tattoo and scuffed black leather
And scans his story. Empty chapters fill it.
Bleak breakfast, coffee, cigarette, the Sun,
His boring job, more cigarettes, more coffee,
Kebab, the petty chatter in the pub,
The late night video, the sweeter smoke
That dopes his dreams, his shallow sleep. The truth
Is what he feels like when he first wakes up.

This human opportunity. We choose.
A pint of lager or a path of bliss?
A dull life's sneering or a naïve attempt?

                        ❧

She gazes at the red-brick hospital's
Religious front, a reverence for illness
Whispering through the silent sliding doors'
Scissors, the in and out of pessimistic pilgrims,
Waving their flower cones to ward off harm.

Her thumbnail scores the rail along the ramp,
Hesitating, a new hostility
To its unholy healing. The mechanics
That measure blips of life, the wires and drips
And striplights in a transit house of birth,
Sickness and death. The slough without the snake.

The tarmac is a soft black trampoline.
A springy snail sits on it, a wooden house
To crawl through, cockpits on the swings to fly,
A ribbed ship like the Dutchman's, a slow slide.

Linda sits on a bench and watches toddlers'
Wobbly haphazardness. An older boy
Climbs up the red ship's rungs. A girl is sliding,
Running round like a second hand for more.
The mothers wait, their hands at rest on empty
Pushchairs, phlegmatic, rushing to the rescue.

She doesn't even want it. The compulsion
And commonness, the stench of milk and nappies.
Why, then? Her feet decided. When she asked, they
Didn't explain, but wandered, walked away.

She was a leaf and leaves are not to blame.
It was the wind, the wind that disobeyed.

ROGER: You know, you only do things when you've got to,
          Last minute essays, right? So I was thinking,
          That's why it's planet critical, the x
          Babies per second, all the shit and concrete.
          It's what we need to make the soul-shift happen.
          It even guarantees it. Or the world
          Will be destroyed, which isn't possible.
          It's like the whole thing's planned. Whoa! Scary
                                          thought.

MARY: It's perfect timing for a global crisis.
          On the millennium.

ROGER: It's such a great
          Coincidence.

MARY: We're lucky we can see it.

ROGER: I think that's what it means to be enlightened.
           It's simple really, all you do is see
           Coincidences, more and more connections,
           The wizard's web.

MARY: The threads of unity.

ROGER: Everyone's looking...

                  Linda interrupts,
         Her shoulders shut, as if it's cold, her eyes
         Oblique. They hold a cordon of concern.

MARY: How did it go?

LINDA: No problem.

ROGER: Great.

                                        A safe
         Re-entry. Just like lying to her parents.

                          ❧

         The guru's old guitar, pale peace signs peeling,
         Already is, he says, a sacred relic.
         He hits it with a busker's heavy twang.
         His faithful fans are nodding sheepishly.

NIRVANA: *The Changing of the Age, my friends,*
         Is the beginning not the end,
         We'll make things new,
         We'll do-ooh-ooh, ooh-ooh-ooh-ooh,
         Whatever God intends, my special friends...

                          ❧

         Werner is unattached to action, though
         Not to its fruits or vegetables. Keith
         Cuts carrots chunkily. His voice, with its
         Falkirk vibrato, is a little motor.

KEITH: This happened last week. Three days in a row!
           It's non-stop cooking.

WERNER: Something must be clearing.
           Some karma.

KEITH: Bollocks.

WERNER: Not accepting it
           Creates more karma.

KEITH: Bollocks.

WERNER: It's a fact.

KEITH: That doesn't mean I like it.

WERNER: No, you shouldn't.
           That's how it works.

KEITH: *That's so amazing*. Show me!

           The chopping board is like a chessboard or
           A field of war. A carrot Kurukshetra.

WERNER: Often the one who serves, the humble cook,
           Is more enlightened than the greatest scholars.
           Think of the Buddha's favourite, Ananda.

KEITH: I said, you'd better help.

WERNER: It's not my karma.

KEITH: Your past life as a carrot?

WERNER: No.

KEITH: Get chopping!

WERNER: I can't. I'm in a capsule of transition.
           It's very delicate.

KEITH: You're always...

WERNER: So?

KEITH: What about me?

WERNER: Ha! Ego shit.

KEITH: Fuck you!

WERNER: I'll tell...

KEITH: I'll stick...

              They see the silence of
Nirvana in the doorway. Not a word.

ૐ

The wise one has a whim. To watch a movie.
It is Saturday night, the crowd of shadows
Is large and loud and lubricated. They,
The seven samurai, without their swords,
Try not to seem too upright in their seats.

An army of Neanderthals attacks
New York and only one man with a 0
.01 chance can stop them. And his wife
Has left him. Corpses in a crossfire. It
Is death at first sight when the hero acts,
The stubborn muscles of his smile like steel.

Nirvana gobbles popcorn from a tub
And gurgles Pepsi from a tank. It is
A guru's second rule. To buy the biggest.
He is a happy child. A god at play.

Mary and Jill sit in the seats of honour,
Next to him, only watching him,
A mirror of the hero, twitching, tensing,
Mouthing his mumble, laughing through his nose.

Like missionaries sent into the jungle,
Roger and Linda squeeze their elbows in,
Suspicious of the armrests on the edge,
Beyond which may be tribes of cannibals.
A fat boy next to Roger slurps his drink
And scrunches popcorn. It is pitiful.
The nuisance and the noise of ignorance.

ૐ

Net curtains, tidemarked yellow, dust-grey, are
Their temple's veil. Nirvana folds a peephole,
Watches the blank road. When a car brakes, he
Exits before it parks.

NIRVANA: I've got a meeting.

          ℤ

Nirvana bows to the black god of cars,
Sits on the back seat. Automatic locks click.
His mother twists to kiss him from the front,
Hands pleading through the cell bars of the headrest.

MRS. STEPHENS: Colin, it's lovely, oh, my...

NIRVANA: Mum...

MR. STEPHENS: Hold tight.

His father puts his foot down with a manly roar.
No soppy scenes, not in a company car.

          ℤ

The restaurant is purple, dim, a boudoir
In an eternal evening, almost empty.
Nirvana pokes his chicken, less distasteful
Than stomaching another of his mother's
Lectures Against The Vegetarians,
Which would remind her...
        If they'd only listen,
Sit at his feet and wonder at his wisdom.
A guru's parents never get the message.

His mother nibbles mini-mouthfuls, gasps
For breath, a dash across a busy road,
Her one-way information superhighway.

MRS. STEPHENS: You need to put some weight on. On your
              cheeks.

It's not a time of year to... Well, that's said.
Your Auntie Maureen sends her love. There's always
Somebody asking how you are. I tell them,
He's doing very nicely. Judith's baby!
That was a scare, thank goodness, little thing.
She's such a pretty... Did you see that programme?
This... What's his name? It's his first book as well
And Robert Redford's bought it for a film!
I thought, that could be... Well, you never know.
You got our postcard? Such a lovely... Oh,
Isn't that waitress just like Rachel? Now…

Nirvana stares down, stabs the dead white bird,
A boyhood structure buckling his shoulders.
His silence is an exile, his resistance
A vacuum that attracts his mother's noise.

His father sucks his steak. An old oak tree
Shading his son, the sapling of his seed,
Though only showing him a frown of bark,
In a male bond of taciturnity.

&

A full-moon freeze chills trances from tight muscles.
The vibes are visible, the gas flames' heat.
The master is a prowling wolf of truth
Amongst his lambs.

NIRVANA: Wrong mind! It's Perfect Light.
        That doesn't mean it's nice or fun or easy.
        No chance! It's Absolute Reality.
        So guess what's needed? Absolute commitment.
        Absolute self-examination. Shit-work.
        It's serious, it's shattering, it's... right?
        So how committed are you? Show your shame.
        What's weak? What's lacking? Keith? He sits there
                                        thinking,
        It isn't me he means. It's you. I know you.
        You're so afraid... He's read the texts, of course,

From Asimov to Zosimos! So what?
You hide behind them. They're your paper walls.
You're terrified of really seeing. Face it,
Find the surrender block, the yes that's no,
The no that's yes. Ask Linda. She's the expert.
The guru sees! Through all your smocks and
                                    sweaters.
The goose is getting fat. Too late for Christmas!
If you were half as hungry for the Truth
As chocolate, you'd be the Truth by now.
Look at you. Like a walrus in a zoo!
Enlightenment means total clarity,
Razor-edged focus, not this bloating blubber.
It's ugly, ugly. Make the sacrifice.
Yes to the Self means no to self-indulgence.
No to more chocolate means yes to Life.
It's why we're here. It's work. It's not a hobby.
So be professional...

ða

An ember tip
Sends wisps of smoke that scent the master's bedroom.
He contemplates the paper prayer of numbers
Stuck to the screen, the cheque his father left him,
Humming a mantra to negate its cost,
Its karma, like a wave that hits a rock.

His eyelids feel a message from his mind
Outside. He floats upstream and finds its source,
Four thousand years ago.
                        The land called Egypt.
He is a pharaoh founding a religion.
Astronomers and slaves salaam his sun-disc,
The palms of wizened eunuchs shade his smile.
He sees a ray, a pyramid of light,
That is his ancestry, his ancient right.

ða

ROGER: I've had this, well, this thought how things could
                                                         change.
           I mean, it's really practical.

JILL: Fantastic.

ROGER: We'll make the Mind of God the Government!
           The best bit is, because we're not a party,
           There'll be no opposition. Just imagine.
           Prime Minister Nirvana.

JILL: King Nirvana!

ROGER: Divine democracy! We'll legislate
           So the whole nation meditates. At work,
           At school. Make churches meditation centres.
           St. Paul's, Westminster Abbey.

JILL: No more hymns!

ROGER: The first step is we'll need to find the money
           To pay for all the candidates' deposits.

JILL: Why don't we say they pay for it themselves?

ROGER: Cover their own seats?

JILL: For the privilege.

ROGER: One man, one vote, it's such a stupid system.
           What about gurus? Or the chosen few?
           No wonder things go wrong, when all that counts
           Is a majority.

JILL: It's not believing.

ROGER: They'll soon need leaders when the Chaos starts.

&

The guru's room, as black as grapes, is clammy
With sex and oil that a snuffed candle had
Heated until it etherised.
                          Nirvana,
His buttocks like a boiling saucepan's lid,
Wobbles on Linda. Heaven is on earth.
He mines her soul-shaft for a ring of gold,

Like a Nibelungen gnome. She grunts in Sanskrit,
Piously praising, pleasing, pushing up.

His belly's flap is spread across her belly.
It kicks. The fatal drum of Zeus's heir.
Her hands are mothering.
                              He shrivels, shaking,
Stumbling to a switch, to bring the light
To Lucifer, her reddened sex-blotched flesh.
She is a naughty child. She blushes. He
Swathes his sarong.

NIRVANA: A bitch! A demon bitch!

He kicks the door wide. Bare bulbs glaring down,
Drowsy disciples hit the light like moths,
Old dressing gowns for wings.

NIRVANA: She lied! She lied!

The foetal Minotaur in Pasiphae.

NIRVANA: Look at her! Fat and stupid! What a bitch!
         This isn't chocolate, it's evil, evil!
         Behind my back! Who knew? I want the truth.
         Mary? You've seen her. Jill? She told you.

JILL: No.

MARY: I never looked.

NIRVANA: You should have!

                              They are puppies
Who have been smacked and slink up loyally.

NIRVANA: Empty her room. We'll lock her there.

                                        ❦

                                    They search it,
Squeezing her mattress for the metal of
A weapon, for a crystal cut across.

They scratch her suitcase for a false compartment,
For a sealed scroll. They sniff her smocks for drugs
And scan her library, her underlinings,
For occult orders. Who is her real master?

Mary and Jill make camp in the damp lounge,
Sorting their own snatched things, with refugees'
Innocent truculence.

❧

          The coverless
Old duvet is a white cocoon. Without
The mattress or the other women's warmth
To help her or her sweaters for a pillow,
Linda is naked, rigid, cold, alone.

Her mind is a steel gangway, loud and narrow,
Suspended in the night. Too shocked to sleep.

A sun of suns irradiates the room,
The same as on that sacred summer day
That showed Nirvana to her. From the wall
A soft white cloud blows. Flowers on the breeze
Ripple a pool of oil.
               A golden child
Is calmly contemplating her. He smiles
And strokes her hair. A spiritual rainbow
Spills from his navel. Lotuses of white
Clouds, blue sky, yellow rays, like English April,
Spill from his higher chakras, that are eyes
In which she sees herself, her bulbous belly,
Reflected, weightless, bathing in his blessing.

❧

The window weeps. The day is foggy grey.
The fire's hiss fries the lounge's sleep-soured air.

64

The guru sits in judge-black robes, stiff-backed,
Humming a broken thunder.
                                        Five disciples,
As lotus-legged as their sore knees allow,
Rattle their throats in raw Tibetan tones.

Nobody looks at Linda. She is glazed,
Out on another morning in her mind.

They meditate on brown stains in the carpet,
Non-human, non-contaminating stains.
The chanting ceases, seven silences,
A void expanding like the universe.

NIRVANA: We see the sin of disobedience,
            Sent by the Old God's system to destroy us.
            She disobeys, deceives us and denies it.
            She lies to hide her lie, she can't stop lying.
            This is the logic of disintegration.
            Think of a sheet. One tiny toe-sized hole
            Tears it in two. Each lie, each why, each no
            Unties us, jams transmission, atomises
            Our unity. It's chaos for the cosmos.
            It cracks the mirror of the Mind of God.
            It's how we'll fail our mission. Don't you care?
            You heard my warning. Why did you ignore it?
            I'm crying in the wilderness again!
            Don't you believe me? Is your faith so feeble?
            Who gave you all your visions, all your bliss?
            Isn't that proof? Or all the truth I've taught you?
            Am I a joke or guru? Tell me!

                        Linda
Stammers, slow words arriving late, her throat
Shaped for another syllable.

LINDA: I'm sorry...
            I don't... I... He's a holy child. He told me,
            Like magic, like my own Annunciation.
            He's really, really special. I can feel him,

He's golden, beautiful, he's here to help us,
He's called the Green Messiah...

NIRVANA: Bullshit! Bullshit!
It's lies again. It's false maternal instinct.
That's why the Old Book's Satan was the most
Beautiful angel. It's the first disguise.
A holy child! If you looked in your womb,
You'd see its pestilence. It's green all right,
A green-skinned tapeworm. It's the sin of pride.
Keeping your special baby. Stupid hubris!
He's poisoned you. A selfish stupid girl!
Linda? *Ad nil*. To nothing backwards. Ha!
How all-important do you think you are?
Well? More important than the Work? Than God?
This world, this little juggling ball in space,
Is bouncing on the brink of its salvation
Or its destruction. If we save it, *if*,
We'll be the princes of the ten dimensions,
But if we fail, when we've been chosen, trusted,
Offered unique technologies by God,
What will our karma be? The ones who knew,
Who could have, nearly did and then forgot.
A karma worse than Judas, worse than Hitler,
A karma that will pay the price in aeons
For the extinction of the Earth forever.
I told you, terminate it.

LINDA: It's too late.

❦

The air is sombre, soft, a windless fall,
As white as ballerinas' tiny tutus
Spiralling in a kingdom of the shades.
Surprises of eternity, in silence,
Snowflakes are moments floating down to earth.

Linda, wrapped in a blanket, breathing out
On wet glass, watches through her prison window.
Gardens collide. Snow mends a broken wall.

The icicles on wires are a cold current,
Flakes on a tree a dust sheet on a nude.

She wants religious history to say,
During the days she calls *Her Tribulations*,
She was so calm she pacified the world
Under an angel's wings. She's so excited.
After the promises, the prophecies,
It's happening, it's serious, it's real.
This time she's not *too little for a big secret*,
Sent to bed early. She's the source, the centre.
It's like a Bible story. And it's her.

Maybe she's being tested by the master,
Her strength of vision, her humility,
To make her worthy of maternity.
She was the one he chose to sow his seed in.

Maybe it's even more incredible.
She's gone beyond the guru, to a truth
He's blind to, truth that's hidden from a man.
That's why he needs her. She's the bearer of
The One Thing Missing From Totality.
Only a holy child can teach the master,
A child who still remembers, a great lama's
Reincarnation, walking from the womb...

The lock clicks. Mary, butting shut the door,
Bringer of lentils, ministers. A bowl,
A mug, a spoon. No knife. She waits until
Linda has licked the bowl clean. Nothing stays.

MARY: There's one thing... Well, I guess I'm curious.
           You never told us you'd come off the pill.

LINDA: I never took it.

MARY: What? You didn't? Gee,
           That's really cheating. Cheating Paul, not me.
           Your guru needs to know.

LINDA: He never asked.

MARY: He trusted you.

LINDA: He never said I should.

MARY: It's basic doctrine. We're symbolic brides.
           Of all his teachings, all the tools he uses,
           Sex with the guru is the highest practice.
           It's tantra, it's the royal route to God
           And you perverted it for procreation.
           It's like he says, a lie conceived a lie.

LINDA: Mary, he's wrong. Just once, the guru's wrong.

MARY: How can you say that?

LINDA: It's the wisdom of
           A mother's mystery. A man can't know.

MARY: He's not a man! You can't be so selective,
           Believing this, ignoring that, like shopping.
           It's all true, it's a whole, it has to be.
           If one thing's wrong, it means that nothing's right,
           But everything we know is right is right,
           Which means it's all right. Right?

LINDA: His child's divine.

❦

The messenger descends from the apostate,
Showing her own faith to the master's court.

MARY: She's on this pregnant power trip, it's weird,
           Like it's her own fertility religion.
           I told her, using reason, nothing heavy.
           She couldn't see it, total tunnel vision,
           Worse than a Christian. Wow! What's really spooky,
           She says the guru's wrong!

                      Nirvana neighs,
           A stale gust of derision through his nose.

NIRVANA: So Linda thinks I'm wrong about the future,
           About the highest states of consciousness,
           About Infinity? Did she explain

Her evidence, her proof? How she received
Divine Omniscience? She's full of shit!
The arrogance of ignorance. So tell me,
Who's with the Guru? Who's with Anti-Guru?
What does it mean? This failure of her faith.
I want to know exactly what you think.

KEITH:　　　It teaches me, I've noticed this before,
The quiet ones, you think they're really holy,
So floaty, so serene, so full of bliss,
All astral-planing, angel choirs, then nothing.
It isn't real. The ones who do the journey,
The solid, stubborn ones, don't wear the haloes.

ROGER:　　　I think... I mean, the future isn't now,
So what we do is always a prediction
Based on the odds. And logically that says
The right choice is to fight what might be evil.
Supposing, right, we fight it and it isn't,
We'd go, *Hey, sorry, seemed a good precaution,*
But if we don't fight and it is... Whoa! Freak-out!
We won't say sorry if the world has ended.

WERNER:　What I think is we're lost in mists of Maya.
Science has proved it. Even solid things
Are empty waves. We think we're sitting still,
We're spinning on the High Speed Spaceship Earth.
Who knows what's true or false? What's right or
　　　　　　　　　　　　　　　　　　wrong?
Only the one who knows what's real, the teacher,
The greatest genius.

JILL:　　　　　　　　　　　　I love my guru.

❧

Dark green, as muddy as the English earth,
Spring is the season of a sacrifice.
Buds wound the bark. It rains.
　　　　　　　　　　　The equinox
Begins with fasting, orders from the master
To sanctify themselves for celebration.

They chant in an incessant aural chain,
Until their mouths hallucinate.
                              Night sinks.
The sweat lodge of the lounge is lit with candles,
Burundi drummers thumping on a tape.

They roast three chickens. Greasy fingers tug
Flesh from the fragile bird bones. Greedy teeth
Tear through the gristle.
                              Juice-smeared Jill and Mary,
Like voodoo bridesmaids, bring down Linda, starved,
Waddling with the world's weight that she bears.
She gnaws two wings at once, a double dinner.

Nirvana, arms wide, is a cross of welcome,
Offering bottles of the cheapest wine.
They swig it, throats raw from the chanting, reeling,
Unused to any alcohol at all.

It is mad March, a festival of fools
Transcending their taboos. A black-tongued goddess
Dances. The drums beat. His initiates,
As blurred as Bacchae, stagger round the room.
He screeches what he teaches.

NIRVANA: Purge it! Punch it!

Keith swipes and sways, a serpent shadow-boxing.
Werner elbows her breast. She yelps and shrinks.

NIRVANA: The belly! Kick the belly!

                              They see scenes
Of medieval karma, burnings, drownings,
Dragging the witch towards the orange gas fire.
Mary and Werner grab her shoulders. Roger
Kicks out. She twists. The victim's victim is
Werner, the kick karateing his groin.
He bleats, as if a big bad boy had burst
His blue balloon. Jill giggles like a gibbon.

ROGER: Stop laughing! Bald head! Brain dead! You're so ugly!

She hits him with a right hook to the jaw.
He sees the light. She squeals and runs round, on
A fun fair, wild with wine, a whirling dervish.

Worship the goddess of hysteria!
She whoops at Werner, pushes Linda, kisses
Mary, spews yellow chicken on a chair.
Linda shakes free. The golden web unthreads.
The guru, ghostly, tiptoes from his throne.

 ❧

The morning sky, as classical and clear
As Raphael, is lapis lazuli.

The artist's sunlight is ironic in
The sick-smeared lounge, the spring day on their skin,
Sleepy and sour, that is as sallow as
A photo on a wrong exposure.
                    Mary
Taps a toe tensely. Keith stands on the threshold,
Wafting the lounge door. Werner, Linda, Jill
Sit waiting.
            Footsteps scuffle down the stairs.
Roger reports, his hands apologising.

ROGER: I knocked. He didn't answer. I went in.
            He's gone, his clothes, his papers, packed and gone!

Mary sucks in the fetid air and shrieks.
Her mouth is blue. A spasm shakes her wrists.
She freefalls.
                Werner punts her to the sofa.
Keith runs for water. Jill and Linda soothe her.
Her breathing sobers to a normal need's
Brave sigh.

ROGER: We'd better split before the rent's due.

LINDA: We can still stay here, search for truth together,
           A group without a guru. Maybe that's
           The New Mind Way. A field of fellowship.
           We'll have a baby avatar to worship...

ROGER: Linda, I don't... I mean, the bread's gone stale.

    A small apocalypse that no one sees
    Is still apocalyptic. Six survivors
    Stare at the desert round the ruined temple,
    At the mirages that were miracles.

LINDA: What'll you do?

ROGER: I don't know. Find some friends.

MARY: I'll call my Mom. She'll mail a ticket home.

JILL: Back to the dreary Druids...

                              Keith is weeping,
    Rigidly, turned to salt. The big drops drip,
    Annoying them, a leaky tap of tears.
    Nobody asks him. They are strangers now.

    Roger runs through the door and up the stairs.
    Werner follows him, his pet wolfhound. Linda
    Waddles out, pats Keith's shoulder, pouting pity.
    Jill fills her rucksack. Mary packs her case.

    Their faith is still the only friend they have,
    Like immigrants who know the guide has tricked them,
    But need to trust him in a strange new city.

                         ❧

    Linda sits on a bus and grips her suitcase,
    Her belly bulging, listening to a girl
    Beg for more crisps. Her mother, hands tied by
    The bags of shopping on her thighs, says no.

    The child looks through the window, simply seeing
    What she can see, inside a rainbow's spectrum.

She isn't searching for a secret, she
Is learning what is out there.
                              Is this it?
These thoughts that are the static of the brain,
The electricity of cells. This whorl
Of genes that is an archaeologist's
Cuneiform scroll, a funeral inscription.
This body that is a reheated meal.
These atoms that are Danaë's hard rain,
The debris of the stars.

❧

            A shadow floats
In a parked car like an aquarium.
Linda plods past it, on a slow suburban
Peace walk. A garden's fringe. A mossy urn.
The street's stones sunbathe in a weekday snooze.

She puts her suitcase down. The baby's weight
Is extra gravity, the earth inside her.
Her gaze drifts like a breeze.
                              The street's trees breathe
Spring warmth, an augury of early blossom
About them. Her smile is the same. A thread
Like silk surprises her. The trees are hers.

She feels the sunlit silence, like new love,
Soaking her soul, an unexpected blessing.
Her palms stroke circles on her swollen womb.
The beauty of the infinite will be
The birthright of her baby. She'll be human.

A European Master

Paris

1996

Critical mass. The crowd attracted here
Is an attraction. More come, crackling,
Like doubts excited by a new idea.
Curious strollers catch the thrill of something,
Teeter on tiptoe.
                    Spotlights splash the night,
Above the stars, like wedding guests, arriving
Outside the cinema. The virgin bride
Strides up the steel-fenced aisle.
                              Her sleek dress is
The slim vase of a single rose, her hair,
November brown, gelled wild, a woodland scene.
A shadow in the well pool of her throat
Trembles. Her high cheeks glint. A string of pearls
Seeds the white scallop of her collar-bone.

The crimson velvet of her lips draws wide,
Like a stage curtain showing eager rows
Of white delight.

PHOTOGRAPHER: Smile please!

                          She smiles more smiles,
Swirling round as a firmament of flash
Shoots from the dark crowd, hawkers' hard-edged cries
Heckling poses.
                    Dizzy from the pleasing,
Julie sees, shaded by the doorway, waiting,
Watching like a proud father, her great groom.
He shrugs and taps his watch.
                              Her gawky grin
Unmasks the art of acting. Sparrow hands
Say sorry to him as she skips inside.

Her face floats on the wall. A green-brown haze
Of distant countryside. *Julie Vidal.*
The Princess Of The Village. Depardieu.

Frescoes of photos frame the open doors.
Galloping horses, cottages in flames,

Julie, mud-smeared, wind-dancing on a mountain,
A midnight wedding's aureole of candles.

A smaller starburst flashes up the line.
The next guest smiles.

❧

     A more substantial calm
Than the slow morning fills the wood-walled study,
Film cans in columns like the ruins of
A Roman temple, white-tagged books. The calm
Created by a concentrating mind,
The way a solemn forest is still silent
Though birds sing. Car hums only heighten it,
The clangs and floor creaks of his upstairs neighbours.

Old posters of his past. Blue rain. *The Lovers.*
Blood in the snow. Black mourners. *Insurrection.*
A Baltic-grey mist. *Exile.* And a frame
That's empty.
    Scripts on shelves. A golden gnome,
Faceless and thin, alone, his foreign Oscar.

Alexis analyses in his armchair
A verse, in French, of an Upanishad.

The true experience of the transcendence
And presence of one's being frees one's mind
From doubt, one's heart from feelings of attachment,
One's life from karma.
     Presence and transcendence.
It must be both, unbounded in the body.

The runes notched in his brow are thoughts. His spine
Is rifle-barrel straight, his short steel hair
Aesthetically austere.
     He twirls the wire
Stalks of his spectacles, conducts the air,

The lenses spotting silver coins of light.

What does it really mean to be that being?
Logic insists our true self is inhuman.
If it's eternal and can be a tree,
An angel or a flea, it isn't human.
There is a human soul, that artists see,
But it is only temporary, like
A stained-glass rose. The real undying light
Shines through it. Or, in theory, it should.
In the Upanishads, it's quick and clear,
Like water springing from a mountain source.
But we're downstream, by a polluted lake.
Is it still possible for us today,
In Paris or wherever, to attain
That state, the timeless omnipresent Self?
We're spiritual novices. Our hearts
Have more attachments than a new computer.
Doubts are the only thoughts our minds believe.
Our egos are urbane and hard. Our freedom
To vote and bloat has atrophied our souls.
What if it isn't possible? We try
Or die. To fail is still to make the journey.

❧

The black style of traditional Japan
Is in the matt shell of the television.
Bodies of light, pulsating, multi-present,
Float in a blue stream. Four philosophers,
Word surgeons, operate on the idea
Of nationality. They agitate,
Their Adam's apples sending their silk ties
Leaping like salmon.
                              Julie, in a niche
Of arm and shoulder, is a woollen walrus
In a big bobbly sweater, Chinese trousers
Washed wan. Vincent leans back, work shirt untied,
Legs sprawled, big feet like Easter Island statues.

79

His free hand finds the keypad, flicks it off.
A black screen.
                      Only closeness. Out of time,
Their breathing bumps together. Lazy noses
Nuzzle. Their senses daydream. Her damp hair's
Wood smoke. The swansdown of his sleeve's white cotton.

VINCENT: Tell me the bad news.

JULIE: What?

                                    He shrugs her shoulders.

VINCENT: In here.

            A torque of tension.

JULIE: No, it's, well,
            A Hollywood producer's seen *The Princess*,
            They're casting…

VINCENT: Why the whisper? That's fantastic!

JULIE: They want to see me. It's a stupid script
            About this evil gang in Eastern Europe
            (It's post-Cold War so they've recast the villains),
            A hero who's American, of course,
            Outnumbered, on a mission, with a gun,
            Etc. etc… And me.

VINCENT: Mass murder with a dash of romance?

JULIE: Right.
            The usual trash.

VINCENT: It's what you need to be
            A star out there. I thought that's what you want.

JULIE: Maybe. I'm not… I've got a chance to choose.
            That's what *The Princess* really means. I'm free.
            I can say no now. Chase the work I want.
            Why should I play their game? It's so degrading,
            So vulgar. That's the waste of time, not waiting
            For real work, films with meaning, with a soul.
            That's it.

VINCENT: No second chateau...

JULIE: Well?

VINCENT: We'll live.

❧

The brown lane is a stained ravine of shade.
Bald sunlight blinks above its precipice.
A waiter deals small dishes like a tarot
Onto a pavement table. Gherkins, pita,
Falafel, hummus, latkes, caviar.

Alexis rips a strip of fluffy bread,
Dips it in purple sauerkraut. His agent,
His pink crown fringed by dandelion hair,
His roll-neck white, his blazer buttoned tight,
Sips his glass, pauses for the taste to pass.

ALEXIS: Antoine, I want to tell you, no more juries,
           No operas, no masterclasses, please.
           Either I find a story for a film
           Or nothing, silence.

ANTOINE: Bergman said that silence
           Is the true inspiration...

                          And on cue
A moped's two-stroke motor whines and splutters.
It scrapes the kerb, skids past the cafe tables
And spurts free.

ANTOINE: Imbecile! It's symptomatic.
           The mental age of this society
           Is adolescent. All the false excitement,
           Thinking it's so important, rushing, rushing.
           Ridiculous!

ALEXIS: The paradox, I think,
           Is that the reason why we live so fast
           Is an anxiety about the future.

81

In an age of stability or sameness,
We're safe, we're slow, we watch the moment
                                                mellow.
But when our future frightens us, what happens?
We rush to meet it!

ANTOINE: It's an itch, a rage,
To do it all before the worst occurs,
To fill the cup.

ALEXIS: But what does it achieve
As truly meaningful experience?
A lot of nothing.

                        In torn skin-tight jeans,
A scooping top, straps showing, a young woman
Steps from a shop, as pretty as she's pleased.

ANTOINE: What a society!

                        She steals his eye
As she struts by, as bouncy as the apples
On Eve's tree.

ALEXIS: Though it's your misfortune too.
Modernity is not your native home.
I see you as an excellent Marquis
Of the Enlightenment.

ANTOINE: No, please, that's awful!

ALEXIS: Why not?

ANTOINE: It's far too decadent for me.
I see myself in Athens in its prime,
With Plato.

ALEXIS: When they sentenced Socrates?

ANTOINE: No...

ALEXIS: When Euripides was forced to write
His psychopathic tragedies? The war
With Sparta was a Balkan civil war.

ANTOINE: It's true we're only really civilised
             In our ideals, but isn't it true too
             That art is weaker in a time of peace,
             When no one needs a masterpiece?

ALEXIS: So now
             Bosnia, even to non-Bosnians,
             Is the *sine qua non* of inspiration.
             I don't know. Can I find an art of peace?

ANTOINE: Like Bach?

ALEXIS: His Passions? Even in the East,
             India's epics are the songs of battles.

ANTOINE: Then I declare a war against today,
             A tragedy of decency and manners,
             Good food and wine!

                    They chuckle, speckled hens
         Clucking over the eggs of their ideas.

                           ❧

         Julie is braced against the phone, its quill
         Combing her hair as she walks to and fro,
         Telling her agent, no to Hollywood.

YVONNE: More of your crazy bullshit! That's your magic,
             Your actress-stardust. It's still crazy, though.
             This is the nineties. No one starves for art.
             We're Spielberg's generation. This is it!
             You're hot till now. These suntanned General
                                    Custers,
             They drive out in their limousines at night,
             You know how many stars are winking at them?
             They're channel-changers, fashion-casters. Catch
                                    them!
             You're not the only actress on the menu.
             It's like a phone book. Flocks of fluffy ducklings
             Flapping their little wings. They're pouting nothings!
             But they'll still get the parts instead of you.

Don't let them! Be the star. You're as rare as Garbo.
You shine, you steal the screen, you're so alive,
Like a light meter, like a lightning rod,
And that's already, when you've hardly started!
What you need now is practice, steady work
Learning your craft, to grow towards that great
Performance, that great film. So when it matters,
You'll be the one they cast. The secret's simple.
Work and you'll work. Say yes and act, act, act.
In good films, bad films. Nothing comes from
                              nothing...
They're flying over soon to check locations.
You can look sullen if you like. They'll think,
She's so mysterious, so very French!
That's what they want. It's supermarket shopping.

❧

Letters from strangers, who have seen his films
In retrospectives, who are now his friends,
From debutant directors, dissertation
Detectives and from actors. Stars of hope.
Alexis clears the leaf fall on his desk,
An old politeness opening them all.

Ambition isn't modest. They are sure
What their fate is, to meet him. They are prophets,
Shouting each other out, the same saint's bone
In sixty shrines.
                    His wife likes to recycle.
He sorts a pile for pulping. Any scripts
Are scribble paper for a friend's young children.

If he lived in a cottage in the woods,
He'd gather storm logs, stoke them in the hearth
And feed their dreams to flames, an ash confetti
The wind would carry to the rocks, the lake,
Like children's letters to Saint Nicholas.

❧

84

Margot leaves two blue glasses, Badoit hissing,
On the low table with her guest.
                              She shakes
A mouse to wake a window on the screen
And ends the sentence broken by the bell.

They can be offhand, they are childhood friends.
Julie lies like a cat and tips a pile
Of art-style magazines. She finds the calm
Insolent monochrome of *Egoïste*.

The stripes of sunlight through the wooden slats
Turn into moonlight in the white apartment,
Shine on the metal oak leaf of the table,
A flat glass bowl, a box of lilac orchids,
Their petals taut, intent as ears to whispers.

Margot kneels on the parquet to be close.

MARGOT: Sorry, it's saved now... On the phone this morning,
        You said, about the sort of parts you're after,
        Maybe it's just the word you used, *worthwhile*,
        I can't help thinking, Maoist film collectives,
        Experimental agitprop…

JULIE: No way!
        I don't like acting to an empty room.
        A film has to compete. Then it confronts us.

MARGOT: I'm not sure that a good film should confront us.
        I don't like social films or issue films
        Or any ideology in art
        That bullies us. It's superficial.

JULIE: No,
        A film that really challenges, that changes,
        Is intimate. It asks us who we are.
        That's what I want, a role that's here, today,
        That shows our souls, our spiritual lives.

MARGOT: But they aren't static, they're dynamic. It's
        A process now. I don't know how you'd film it.

JULIE: Neither do I.

MARGOT: Is therapy a story?
            Is meditation? They're routines, they're not
            Dramatic action, they're a private path.

JULIE: It's like imagining imagination...

MARGOT: Although... The golden role for any actress
            Is the romantic oracle. It's gazing
            At your own soul. Why change the archetype?
            Be a new muse.

JULIE: The same old thing?

MARGOT: It's timeless.
            The right director finds you, falls in love...

JULIE: Margot!

MARGOT: It's art. He's hopelessly inspired.

JULIE: I don't want an affair.

MARGOT: So keep it pure,
            Seduce his eyes aesthetically, torment him,
            Then consummate it... On the screen.

JULIE: That's better.

MARGOT: It's love, though. Only love can show the soul.

JULIE: So tell me who he is, this great director,
            My cinematic soulmate?

MARGOT: Really?

JULIE: Yes.

MARGOT: Alexis Vasary.

JULIE: Don't tell my agent!
            His last film was the worst film in the world.

MARGOT: I think I missed it.

JULIE: *Freedom Means Bananas.*
            It was a comedy. It wasn't funny.

MARGOT: But *Insurrection, Exile...*

JULIE: *Truth Of Man.*
        Of course. They're masterpieces. Of the Eighties.
        Since then, he's stopped. One flop, five years of
                                        nothing.

MARGOT: Waiting for you...

JULIE: He's Lazarus, I'm not
        Religious.

MARGOT: Don't you want to re-inspire him?
        Homecoming, Truth Of Woman, Resurrection.
        His new artistic anima?

JULIE: Not me.

MARGOT: Who else is there? A true creator now?

᪣

When you've been married twenty seven years,
Love is a fact.
            Alexis chews the gristle
Of yesterday's baguette, its broken crust
Crunching under their breakfast bowls of coffee.
Vera, his wife, cuts slices of an apple.
Their teenage children, Orson and Colette,
Slump at the table, slurping, semi-surly,
Especially so early in the day.

ALEXIS: What was the film like?

ORSON: Junk!

COLETTE: You wouldn't like it.

ALEXIS: Not if it's junk.

ORSON: It's cool junk…

COLETTE: You're too old.

VERA: Colette!

COLETTE: You'd love it, Mummy.

ORSON: No, she wouldn't.

ALEXIS: I don't think I'm the target audience.

ORSON: You've got to see it…

ALEXIS: If you say so.

VERA: Orsie,
            About the weekend, have you changed your mind?

ORSON: I don't like plans.

COLETTE: That's what your teachers say!

Colette and Orson run to classes. Vera
Walks to the charity for migrants' rights
Where she translates.
                          Alexis is alone.
He sweeps the table's crumbs off with his hand,
Sponges the dishes in a bowl's hot foam
And buffs them dry, a butler's eye for detail.

He sits and reads *Le Monde*. The world, the world…
This Roast Beef Madness is a British tantrum
In Brussels. Will the single currency
Precipitate a second '68?
A war in Africa. More unemployment.
A Lille drug dealer dead in jail. The sale
Of prostitutes from Moldova to Paris.
A gangland bomb in Moscow. The proposed
EU expansion to the East. A praised
Production of *The Cardinal Of Dublin*.
An in-depth interview with Demi Moore.

His thumb and finger are a beard of thought.
He contemplates his desk. A pipe of pens.
A pad of paper with the blue grid that
He can't get used to. Pebbles from the Baltic.
A snapshot from the summer he met Vera.

Work or a walk? A walk is always good.
He zips his jacket, juggles keys and goes.

&

The small soft-spoken bookshop's ship-grey shelves
Are soothing on the eye, the cream and white
Mosaics of novels on the tables too.

Alexis reads the titles on the spines
Along a row of poetry. He opens
A book, like a bird's wings beating, stops it flying.

A new translation offers him its notes
Of something unachieved. A film's first draft.
He queues to pay.
                    The tall proprietor
Is criticising prizes, the Goncourt
And others, with an old man who once won one.

Julie is queuing too. She turns for help
And sees Alexis. Is that really him?
Like a Giacometti bird in his black jacket,
Patient, possibly entertained, a brief
Book in his hand. Her own book leapfrogs free.

JULIE: Excuse me... Mr. Vasary?

                              His eyes
Glint through his glasses, grey brows in a crimp
Of impish questioning.
                              Her anxious grin
Has the same artless grace to it again.
He thinks about the saying, *imperfection
Adds to perfection.* She is so sublime,
Her broad mouth like a plum, her ski-slope nose,
Her shoulders like a heron. She's an actress.
It's obvious. The thought-translucent skin.
The blankness of an empty picture frame
In which an unknown portrait can be shown.

He nods. He doesn't smile. He is directing.

They sit beneath an orange awning, in
A grove of cane chairs, brass hoops round the marble
Tables, a brown froth drying on their cups.

ALEXIS: In 1989, I'm not complaining,
 But I became an artist of the past.
 The transformation when the Wall collapsed
 Created a completely new aesthetic.
 Before the Fall! It was an innocence,
 An innocence through evil, so to speak,
 A bleak simplicity. The whole of Europe
 Lived in the shadow of a monolith,
 Which made its artists monolithic too
 Or monumental, maybe. When we filmed
 That state of stasis, we showed something timeless.
 The metaphors were meaningful, were clear.
 A numbness, separation, exile in
 A wintry world of purity and grandeur.
 Thank God it's gone! But it was universal.
 Seeing an actress on a rainswept beach
 Staring at iron waves, you knew the reason.
 The symbol was as strong as snow in haiku.
 That was the way we showed the soul, through
            sorrow,
 Mournfully. Then the winter turned to spring.
 The ice thawed. Slush and mud and buds and
            blossom
 On blighted trees. The chaos of today!
 The loss of tragedy was good for life,
 But bad for art. I still can't see an image.
 It's too confused, too quick, too small. The stuff
 Of prophecy or wisdom isn't there.
 What was romantic has become rococo,
 Banal and bourgeois. Well... I tried to film it
 When it first started. *Freedom Means Bananas.*
 It was a failure.

JULIE: Won't you try again?

ALEXIS: We were the holy innocents, they said.
 That was the East, but in the West as well

There was another sort of innocence,
Without a past, an art that was adopted
From Hollywood. That's changing too… You're
                                pleased?
What is our genealogy? Old Europe!
We grub its earth for roots like starving peasants,
But those old roots are stunted, they're as bitter
And black and vicious as the Balkans teach us.
There's subject matter there, but not for me,
There's too much risk. And I'm uprooted here.
I've even lost the meaning of an exile,
Now I just live abroad.

JULIE: You won't go home?

ALEXIS: We've thought about it… No, it wouldn't work.
Our children's home is here. And, anyway,
I'm not a local artist.

JULIE: Not at all,
But maybe what you're looking for is wrong.
A monolithic concept of the Zeitgeist?
A single angel's wing above us all,
The soul of Europe!

ALEXIS: Possibly. It's true
We've scattered, little castles of the nations,
A middle-Europe multiplicity.
Though, thankfully, the souls who live here now
Are global. Arabs, Asians, Africans.
They'll save us from the curse of atavism,
That's what my wife believes, her big crusade.
Well… Are you married?

JULIE: No. We live together.

ALEXIS: Is he an actor?

JULIE: He's a doctor.

ALEXIS: Good.

JULIE: It seems to me, if things are so fragmented,
Instead of films that universalise,
Grand and romantic, you should focus on

Something that's small, a more specific story
Of ordinary life.

ALEXIS: It isn't easy,
Unless you make an ordinary film,
A boring slice-of-life. It needs a theme,
A story, if you like, a mood, a style,
That really resonates, so it creates
Something profound, a cinematic language
Of spiritual truth... But maybe you
Can find a story for me. Something new.

JULIE: An ordinary story of the soul...

ALEXIS: And with, of course, a starring role for you!

Julie and Margot are intriguing in
A chic Zen café, noses almost meeting
Over a tiny table's formal garden
Of rice and salad bowls, a shoyu inkpot.

JULIE: I don't know what he wants. Or what he means.
              A story of the soul?

MARGOT: Well, what's your own?
              That's what he wants.

JULIE: My soul?

MARGOT: It could be worse...

JULIE: Haha! He doesn't care whose soul it is,
              As long as it's a story that's inspiring.
              Mine would be boring.

MARGOT: Shall we show him mine?

JULIE: Soul by Armani!

MARGOT: Catch that cat!

JULIE: Me? Ow!

MARGOT: So what's the plan?

JULIE: I'm searching for a plot.

MARGOT: A spiritual story?

JULIE: That's the problem.

MARGOT: I think you need to find your own soul's first.

JULIE: Maybe. That's still a problem.

MARGOT: No, it isn't.

JULIE: Here we go. Learn to meditate?

MARGOT: At last!

JULIE: I'd rather not.

MARGOT: It's not the only way.
          You could wait for an accident of grace
          Or what they call the yoga of disaster
          Or a near-death escape, they're mystical.
          Whatever's to your taste. Or a technique.

JULIE: I'll think about it... Which would you suggest?

MARGOT: Samadhi meditation would be easy.
          It's Westernised, mild-mannered, not too weird
          And well-attended. Even actors go there.
          You might meet an old cast friend.

JULIE: Please! I'd need
          Something that's more discreet.

MARGOT: Haha! Okay.
          There's one I'd recommend, it's small but nice,
          Called Brahmananda Yoga.

❧

                    Curtains shut,
        As if a film is screening in his study,
        Alexis sits, his eyes shut too, arms folded,
        His spectacles a spider on his desk.

        His intuition is a silent film.
        He sees stars in the gaps of broken streetlamps,
        A gutter's rusty stream on oil-black cobbles,
        A disused church, its windows planked, its door

93

Unhinged and splintered.
                        He can go inside.
A rain hole in the roof invites the sky.
Weeds creep across the stones. The blanks of stolen
Icons are their ghost-negatives.
                        The night
Is re-enshrining sanctity through starlight.

It is an image only to imagine.

&

The bridge across the Seine is Janus-faced.
The east side is restored, bold black and gold
Lanterns and iron Empire beasts, the west
Moody and muted, flaky verdigris.

Julie leans on the rail. The sun's Seurat
Stipples the river. Bateaux mouches slide by.
She is a child whose parents are insisting,
While all her friends are playing in a park,
She starts her first piano lesson now.
And this is an invisible piano,
Which, if it does exist, will only play
Silence, a song of never-ending calm.
What's wrong with Mozart? Why not soak her senses
In fiction, in a film, in something real?

&

The wind threads cool surprises through the loft's
Saluting windows. Treetops toss and tremble
Against the slates and shutters.
                        Incense stains
The airy space. A tinsel garland gilds
A photo of a guru. Fourteen guests
Sit on fat cushion balls, in pastel cottons.
Their silence has a synergy, a strong
Stillness, a slow film showing frame by frame.

Julie sits by the doorway, straight and steady,
In her new role, an actress imitating,
And feels the downward force of it around her,
As if the loft is pressurised.
                              The wind
Blows thoughts across her face, odd lists of questions.
She feels rogue itches, random throbs.
                                    A light
Shines through her eyelids, a soft aureole,
Like butter lamps or firelight on brocade,
The glow of the poetic cloth of gold.

       ❧

A meadow's scent wafts off a mug of tea,
Too hot to sip. Julie sits, chin on knee,
Hugging her calves, and listens to a woman
Stooping towards her with an equine grin,
Whose wiry hair keeps spilling, interrupting
Her easy chatter with a new acquaintance.

ANNE: Wait, let me guess, a teacher?

JULIE: I'm an actress.

ANNE: I'm sorry, I don't recognise you, I
           Don't go to films now.

JULIE: No? Is there a reason?

ANNE: I don't like seeing negativity.

JULIE: Well, it…

ANNE: I'll introduce you to Sandrine.
           She used to be an actress too.

JULIE: It's hard…

ANNE: She stopped when it conflicted with her practice.
           It was a life-choice.

JULIE: What does she do now?

ANNE: Something in advertising. She can tell you.

JULIE: So what attracted you to try this path?

            We store a set of speeches to explain,
            Shaped before sleep, selected, simplified,
            Synopses of the secret text of truth.

ANNE: My parents were old-fashioned atheists,
            Good communists, my father was like Stalin,
            And I was their indoctrinated daughter,
            A protest junkie. I was so irate
            At how the masses got exploited, the
            Capitalist cabals that controlled the world,
            I couldn't cope. I chain-smoked, drank, popped pills.
            Anti-depressants, tranquillisers... Useless!
            What was I? A consumer of neuroses,
            Totally alienated from the life
            I marched for. Then, in 1989,
            My world collapsed. It's weird, I can't explain it,
            Even my parents weren't pro-Soviet,
            But it was psychological. I watched
            A trick of history, for no real reason,
            Abolish my ideal. The dream was over.
            I woke up, lonely, in the dead of night...
            Then a friend dragged me to a meeting here.
            I can't describe how cynical I was,
            How hard. My mind was totally defended.
            So the truth simply stole into my heart!
            I started breathing, smiling, feeling happy,
            Seeing a life inside. I realised
            This was the first time I had changed the world,
            The bit of it that's me. So now when I
            Help at a children's charity, it's pure,
            From joy, not anger. It's a Sunday hobby,
            That's all. I do more good just sitting here.
            This is what's really revolutionary!
            It's taught me something truly beautiful,
            I mean, that liberty, equality,
            Fraternity aren't principles on paper,
            They're the three primal principles of life.
            We *are* all free, eternally, uniquely,

In our unbounded beings. We're all one,
The highest, most sublime equality,
All Brahman. And we know, we feel each other
In an amazing union of love.
We meditate. We sow these seeds of light
In our own global consciousness...

❧

Alexis

Listens to Julie's long soliloquy.
The café table is a small round stage.

The words are a fresh fountain in her throat,
Her cheeks are red, her eyes as bright as stars.
He waits a moment while her echo dies.

ALEXIS: We're playing chess. Your white knight has advanced.
My black rook counters. After Brahmananda,
Your guru, had anointed a young heir
And died, the new god-master turned his taste
To teenage girls and secret bank accounts,
Which, after all, the Absolute includes.
A putsch took place. A purer monk took charge,
Claiming he'd always been the true successor,
And what was past was airbrushed to perfection,
Like Stalin cleaning Trotsky from the truth.
I think that's even worse than decadence.
The choice is simple, honesty or power,
And they chose power. Out of a devout
Obsession with their mission, I agree,
But that's why it's a rigid institution,
They stopped it being fearless, being real.

JULIE: I don't know all the history behind it,
But what they do is real. The teaching works.
It's wonderful!

ALEXIS: I wouldn't say it's worthless,
But it opposes you outgrowing it.

It can't allow the honest confrontation
That frees us from the ego and its fear.

JULIE: I'm only a beginner, I don't know,
But they believe you don't need to confront things,
Simply surrender.

ALEXIS: To the teacher's will?
It turns the true authority of wisdom
Into authoritarian abuse.
Not questioning, obsession with perfection,
A power politics of purity
Corrupts them all, these guru corporations.
They're crawling over Eastern Europe now,
Like travelling bordellos of the soul!

JULIE: So why not make a film about it?

ALEXIS: No,
I wouldn't want my work to publicise
Their problems, that's the prejudice already.
I want to film a free experience,
An innocence of exploration.

JULIE: Mine!
What's wrong with it? It's innocent, it's real.

ALEXIS: The weakness is what works is a technique.
On screen, it seems a trick, it isn't earned.
Hollywood shows us miracles. They're easy,
Special effects. A real one, though, is when
An audience can sense it in their souls.
It needs dramatic action, meaning, true
Emotion. That's what causes all catharsis.

JULIE: You mean a film can't show what's real?

ALEXIS: That's right.
It shows a metaphor, of actors, sets,
Of cinematic style, and it's alive,
It works, not if it simulates what's real,
But if it's faithful to that metaphor.

JULIE: Maybe the metaphor needs changing.

ALEXIS: Always!
            But what's the new one? What's the filter for it,
            The frame, the focus, the aesthetic fit,
            To give this new condition of the soul,
            Whatever we may call it, modern Europe,
            Its comedy of possibilities,
            The awe of its analogy on film?
            Honestly, I don't know.

&

                    An orange segment
    Of sunset gets more gaudy as its angle
    Gets more acute.
                    According to Vincent,
    Relationships need rules, which must be easy
    To be effective. *Never let a woman
    Iron your shirts.* He points a jet of steam,
    Presses a cuff, finesses the steel blade,
    Like D'Artagnan, a laundry musketeer.

JULIE: So then he asked me if I'd like to see
            The Gallery of Peace's exhibition,
            Traditions of Tibet, its sacred scrolls.

VINCENT: And you said, *Yes, my boyfriend wants to see that,
            We're free on Sunday.*

JULIE: No...

VINCENT: So when's the date?

JULIE: A date! What are you thinking?

VINCENT: He's a man,
            A middle-aged romantic, a director...

JULIE: He wouldn't dare. He's too fastidious.

    He folds the flattened shirt and adds it to
    A white week on a chair, his calendar.
    The musketeer unplugs his burning sword.

99

VINCENT: At least he tells the truth when he's seducing.
         Pop! He dismissed it.

JULIE: He's a dissident.

VINCENT: Thank you, Vasary. We can stop rehearsing
         The Happy Hindu...

JULIE: Don't be patronising!

VINCENT: You don't believe it?

JULIE: No, you disbelieve it.
         I'm more empirical. I've tried it, proved it.

VINCENT: And you're the artist? It's imagination,
         A mental compensation for not seeing,
         Like dreaming.

JULIE: I suppose you're so reductive
         Because you're scientific? You're just jealous.
         You're whining like a little boy left out.

VINCENT: Reductive? I won't oversimplify
         Your psychological complexity...
         Of course, the mind has spiritual states,
         But they're discrete, they're thoughts and thoughts
                                        are private,
         They don't exist outside the mind.

JULIE: You think
         Nothing exists outside your own mind...

VINCENT: Me?
         Who acts here? The professional solipsist!

JULIE: The great romantic doctor knows it all!
         He sticks his stethoscope against my heart,
         Thump, thump, he's an authority on love!

The Infinite Compassion Bodhisattva,
Tibet's sublime protector, smiles at them.
His arms are a thousand clouds, his palms are a thousand
                                        flames.

A ring of Taras, lilies on a lake
Around him, are his teardrops for the world.

The faded scroll is an evangelist,
A dharma-bringer in the smart white space.
Art guards patrol, belt radios like pistols.

ALEXIS: The true test is to feel compassion for
            China. That's why they hate the Dalai Lama.
            His moral victory.

JULIE: I just feel angry.
            The temples, people, even its poor wildlife,
            It's like an inventory of the evil
            That's possible on Earth.

ALEXIS: Our Governments
            Forgive them too. At least we tried the Nazis.
            Now we sign trade agreements. Or, like us,
            We pay to see displays of stolen art.
            The Chinese sold these treasures to the West.

A pastoral of meditating monks,
In red robes, with a laughing lion near them,
A river singing melodies of mantras
Between green hills.

ALEXIS: It's heightened, but it's true,
            It was a sanctified society,
            With all the inner arsenal of peace,
            Enlightened lamas and a ring of mountains,
            Even in simple self-defence a fortress.
            It should have been as safe as Switzerland,
            But they were too complacent, too corrupt,
            And all the meditation in Tibet
            Couldn't keep out the Communist invasion.

A wheel of torments round a mandala,
The victims yelling, entrails chewed by dogs,
Lynched on a branch that blossoms, charred, impaled.

ALEXIS: What does it mean? The Buddhist platitude
           Is karma. In the West, it's even worse,
           Computer-simulated complex systems,
           Without the simple feeling of a purpose.
           It's true that needing meaning is a weakness,
           Like telling children that it's safe to sleep.
           But I'm inquisitive. A search for it
           Structures my work. It's why my films exist.
           I always want to meet the mystery,
           To hear the holy heart of harmony.

      A scarlet goddess dances on a sun-disc,
      Drinking a conch cup's blood, as beautiful
      As thunder, shaking tangled snakes of hair.
      Her servants stand around her, holding lanterns,
      With ribbons of black prayers that flutter as she dances.

ALEXIS: It's a dark bridge to cross. But the Tibetans
           Don't share our guilty gloom. Their piety
           Is cheerful, earthy, sturdy. They accept
           Misfortune as an element of fortune,
           The mixture of the inexplicable.

❧

      Vincent is slicing slivers of tomato.
      His sister stirs a pot, its steaming stew
      Snarling up at her.
                     Garance, his little niece,
      Snuggles against her almost-aunt. Julie
      Whispers a story, pictured on the page,
      The Princess Who Was Never Satisfied.

JULIE: *And so she rode home on the same white pony.*
           She saw the wheat fields waving in the wind
           To welcome her, the blushes on the fruit trees,
           The castle's open gate. She saw her father
           Rushing to meet her, crying as he kissed her.
           She was so tired, she climbed up to her bedroom.
           It hadn't changed, her wooden box of toys,

102

Her doll with one arm broken on the pillow.
It was the best girl's bedroom in the world.

She runs her fingers in a fairy tale
Through the girl's curly hair.

GARANCE: You read so nicely.
          Why don't I see you on the television?

JULIE: You've seen me in the video I gave you.

GARANCE: Not on the programmes I watch.

JULIE: Would you like that?

GARANCE: I'd tell my friends!

JULIE: You shouldn't boast about it.

GARANCE: I don't know why you're famous. No one knows
                                                    you.

≥

The sun's glare ricochets off the white lips
Of the boats' basin. Statues' shadows are sticks.
Readers of novels languish in the heat,
Their three-chair trick above the Jardin's dust.

A chess school broods like hunchbacks in the shade,
A falcon of fingers pouncing on a pawn.
The lime trees, with their white-green grey-green leaves,
Are music stands where flocks of finches trill.

Julie sees how Alexis, fully focussed
On arguing, absorbs the scene around him,
Filing the filmic lines for future use.

ALEXIS: I think the way to show the soul today
            Would be by all its qualities. Compassion,
            Coincidence, serenity, seclusion.
            A quiet beauty. A light-hearted laughter.
            That's not enough, though. In the mausoleum
            We lived in, we were solemn, we were silent.
            The Cold War was a continent of fear.

103

One glimpse of the existence of the soul
Was an artistic victory! But now
We're living in a marketplace. What use
Are glimpses? Isolated accidents!
We need to see the path, the art of it,
The inner pilgrimage, in our apartments,
In offices and parks. You've shown me how
It opens. An interior of light,
Like dawn. But the development is harder.
It's secret, slow, a tunnel to the truth.
And how would we describe the resolution,
The new beginning of enlightenment?
On film? A rainbow bridge above our heads,
A white screen underneath a stream of dreams...
I don't want to be allegorical,
The medieval Grail, a myth of Vishnu,
The distance means it's easy to dismiss it.
The boldest style would be an innocent
Naturalism, showing that it's real,
But all you'd see would be the surface of it.
It needs to be translated to a story,
But what that story is, I couldn't say,
I'm sorry.

JULIE: Aren't you stopping the idea
By over-analysing it?

ALEXIS: Perhaps.
I used to film the things I couldn't film…
I'm older now, removed from it and, well,
To tell the truth, directing is depressing.
The muddy mornings, the money, shouting, selling.
I won't do it again unless I'm sure,
Unless it's something inescapable.
For you, though, you're an actress, you're more agile.
Films come and go more quickly, with a role's
Reincarnation, up and down, the karma
Of casting! And you're young, you should be
                                        working,

Across your range. Romantic comedy
Would suit your style, the lightness of your spirit.
It's an equivalent intoxication.
Let's hope a Europhile American
Director gets the green light for a Nineties
Remake of *Roman Holiday*!

JULIE: I hope so!
I used to wish that I was Audrey Hepburn.

That gawky grin's goodbye, her big warm eyes'
Affectionate appreciation and
She walked away. A buggy blocked his view.

Alexis, in his study's sanctum, reads
A poem, its lines like a tracking shot.

*The rain runs down the window pane. The pane
Projects the room and she is in the rain.*

The pane is what allows it. In and out
Are seen through what's between. He marks the margin.

An actor's eyes. They shut. We see the soul.
They open and we see the world around them.
A woman's life. Internal and external.
That's the dynamic of it. In and out.
Which means it doesn't matter what she does.

She meditates already, so it's not a
Deus ex machina, it's incidental.
She's no one's devotee, so she's a free
Protagonist. It doesn't sell solutions.
It's intimate, mysterious.
                              The soul?
We see her inner world. An incandescence?
A cave inside her skull? A dreamery?
What are the faces of the figures in it?
They're casual, elusive, post-religious,

The blue-skinned goddesses of tolerance.
Should it show psychodramas of her past?
The squash of birth, the giant land of childhood,
Though not as flashbacks, as dissolving dreams.

Not only when she meditates. Whenever
Her eyes shut. On the Metro. In a park.
In a hot bath. Before she sleeps. A concert.
The music floats between what's in and out.

Is it a comedy? The gifts of grace
That are so minor, so meticulous,
They're funny. Is she clumsy? Solitary?
A party she says no to. What her friends
Think of her. She's distracted, diffident.
Those sensibilities that are too subtle
To say.
        Like Dostoyevsky's *Idiot*?

What is her work? Not in the arts. Does it
Cost her her job? She gets one lower paid,
Less pressured.
                Does her boyfriend disbelieve her?
They argue. Does she end it? She's alone.

Why do we care about her? She's sincere,
Impulsive, open-hearted, innocent.
Self-absorbed? Yes, but not an egotist.

What do we want to know? What keeps us watching?
We need to feel the force of what she does,
To be intrigued what its effect will be.
We need to see the value of it too,
The way it energises and enlivens.

The title? *Pilgrim*? *Silence Of The Heart*?
We see her inner vision isn't closed
Or cloistered, it's unbounded, inundated,
Like angels dancing on a pin. An image
Creates another image, more and more,
Which alters whose experience it is.

She blinks. We see a silver web of souls
Unconsciously communicating. Strangers
Scattered round Europe. Scenes of all their lives?
Superimpose a hall, a hut, a chapel?
Which means it's a polyphony, a collage.
Democracy?
                Tibetan-Spanish Buddhists.
A Russian mystic. A young Polish mother
Praying, the candle flames' wax tears of joy.
A hoarse old man, Bengali-British, chanting.
A Berlin yoga student's smooth samadhi.

The first frame is a white-gold opalescence,
A formlessness that slowly focuses
As something opening. We see through her
Eyelashes early sunlight in a room.
She grunts and stretches.
                      Ash specks on the lace
Of an altar cloth. Her icons are eclectic.
A fallen prayer shawl straggles like a coastline.
She sketches makeup, zips her office dress,
Stuffs papers in a satchel and sprints out.

What is her arc? A gradient of feeling?
Or something grander? Universal love?

What is her name? She's French. Irène? Delphine?
She lives in Paris. Or she lives in London?

What is the ending? Opening or shutting?
Or neither? She sees in and out the same.

A Georgian Anthology

Andrew Staniland's *A Georgian Anthology* is a sequence of poems inspired by the classical myths about Prometheus and Colchis, by Georgia's own mythology and history, by its poetry, especially Shota Rustaveli's *The Knight In The Panther Skin*, and by the beauty of the Georgian landscape, with its castles, towers, monasteries and the mountains of the Caucasus.

Letters Of Introduction (2018)

Andrew Staniland's *Letters Of Introduction (2016)* includes a series of odes, four *Sonnets On Public Life* and a series of *Three-Line Variations* that are an English lyrical equivalent of *haiku*. There are poems about post-truth politics and #MeToo, as well as poems about Armenia, written before the April 2018 revolution, including a sequence, *Thirty-Nine Letters*, that has a poem for each letter of the Armenian alphabet.

PLAYFUL POEMS (2016)

Andrew Staniland's *Playful Poems (2016)* is a sequence of over a hundred short poems written between March 2015 and August 2016 and prompted by reading most of Shakespeare's plays in their likely chronological order. There are poems about the wars in Ukraine and Syria, refugees, dictators, nationalism and Brexit, as well as *The lovely wood of piebald light/That any English poem is.*

RHAPSODIES (2014)

Andrew Staniland's *Rhapsodies (2014)* takes its title from the verse form of the two long poems at its centre, *Rhapsody* and *Corona Lumina,* written in long rhyming couplets. The same verse form is used for a poem about the Ukrainian musicians *Dakh Daughters* and Valentin Silvestrov. There are translations from Russian and Ukrainian, a tribute to Seamus Heaney and a sequence of short poems about an album by the French singer-songwriter Amélie-les-crayons.

THE PERENNIAL POETRY (2010)

Andrew Staniland's *The Perennial Poetry (2010)* is a collection of contemporary English Romantic poetry written in classical metre. There are poems about spiritual experience, creativity, love and poetry itself. The subjects include contemporary films and paintings, Chartres cathedral and the war in Afghanistan, a trip to Tallinn and writing a themed poem for a poetry competition. There are odes and sonnets, including translations of French, Spanish, Italian and German sonnets.

Two Story Poems (2009)

Andrew Staniland's *Two Story Poems (2009)* are original stories in classical verse. *A Human Disguise* is a spiritual comedy set in ancient India. A minor god takes on human form to hide from a demon who is chasing him. *Compassion* is a ghost story set in medieval Japan. A *samurai* gains a supernatural power that is too terrible for him to use.

HYMNS, FILMS AND SONNETINAS (2007)

Andrew Staniland's *Hymns, Films And Sonnetinas (2007)* are written in classical metre, in the romantic tradition of English poetry. They include *Five Hymns* (dedicated to five gods and goddesses representing different elements of contemporary culture and spirituality), *Twelve Films By Eric Rohmer*, *An Older Actress* (a narrative poem in alexandrine couplets about a French actress and her film career), *William Blake And The Eighteenth Century New Age* and *Sonnetinas* (a miscellaneous sequence of sonnet-like miniatures).

NEW POEMS (2006)

The poems in Andrew Staniland's *New Poems (2006)* are poems about contemporary spiritual experience, written in classical metre, in the romantic tradition of English poetry. They include a series of odes and a sequence of short poems which give the collection its title.

THE BEAUTY OF PSYCHE (2005)

Andrew Staniland's prose-poem novel *The Beauty Of Psyche (2005)* is a retelling of the Greek myth of Cupid and Psyche as a novel about imagination. The characters are played by actors, against a backdrop of paintings, models and sets. The story at times becomes a series of paintings and sculptures in an exhibition. And the references to people, films, theatre and other myths may or may not be imaginary too.

THE WEIGHT OF LIGHT (2004)

Andrew Staniland's prose-poem novel *The Weight Of Light (2004)* is a lyrical description of the inner life and spiritual practice of Delphine, a Frenchwoman living in London. It is set entirely in her apartment, like a camera recording the poetry of her daily life, her meditations and spiritual experiences. It is a "new spirituality" novel that is both literary and an honest description of a contemporary spiritual life.

Three Cine-Poems (1997)

The three cine-poems collected here use classical blank verse and contemporary cinematic narrative techniques to tell their stories.

White Russian (1995) is a lyrical description of a young Russian woman's life in London.

A Child Of God (1996) is a comic study of a New Age guru and his small band of devotees.

A European Master (1997) is a debate about contemporary aesthetic values between a French actress and an East European film director.

POEMS (1982-2004)

This is a collection of Andrew Staniland's poems from 1982 to 2004. Some are written in free verse, some in metric verse. They are in the romantic tradition of English poetry and explore contemporary spiritual and psychotherapeutic experience.

Four Plays (1994)

The Temple Of The Goddess (1992) is a verse tragedy set in pre-classical Greece. A matriarchal bronze age state is invaded by a patriarchal iron age army.

The Playwright (1993) is a drama about resurgent nationalism in post-communist Eastern Europe.

Mornings In The Life Of A Theatre Critic (1993) is a London theatre comedy.

The Valley Of Stones (1994) is a tragedy of survival and defiance in a refugee camp.

www.ingramcontent.com/pod-product-compliance
Lightning Source LLC
Chambersburg PA
CBHW031151130726
47988CB00006B/2626